The Public Enemy

Wisconsin/Warner Bros. Screenplay Series

The Public Enemy

Edited with an introduction by

Henry Cohen

Published for the Wisconsin Center for Film and Theater Research by
The University of Wisconsin Press

Published 1981

The University of Wisconsin Press
114 North Murray Street
Madison, Wisconsin 53715

The University of Wisconsin Press, Ltd.
1 Gower Street
London WC1E 6HA, England

First printing

Printed in the United States of America

For LC CIP information see the colophon

ISBN 0-299-08460-4 cloth; 0-299-08464-7 paper

Publication of this volume has been assisted by a grant from
The Brittingham Fund, Inc.

Contents

Foreword

In donating the Warner Film Library to the Wisconsin Center for Film and Theater Research in 1969, along with the RKO and Monogram film libraries and UA corporate records, United Artists created a truly great resource for the study of American film. Acquired by United Artists in 1957, during a period when the major studios sold off their films for use on television, the Warner library is by far the richest portion of the gift, containing eight hundred sound features, fifteen hundred short subjects, nineteen thousand still negatives, legal files, and press books, in addition to screenplays for the bulk of the Warner Brothers product from 1930 to 1950. For the purposes of this project, the company has granted the Center whatever publication rights it holds to the Warner films. In so doing, UA has provided the Center another opportunity to advance the cause of film scholarship.

Our goal in publishing these Warner Brothers screenplays is to explicate the art of screenwriting during the thirties and forties, the so-called Golden Age of Hollywood. In preparing a critical introduction and annotating the screenplay, the editor of each volume is asked to cover such topics as the development of the screenplay from its source to the final shooting script, differences between the final shooting script and the release print, production information, exploitation and critical reception of the film, its historical importance, its directorial style, and its position within the genre. He is also encouraged to go beyond these guidelines to incorporate supplemental information concerning the studio system of motion picture production.

We could set such an ambitious goal because of the richness of the script files in the Warner Film Library. For many film titles, the files might contain the property (novel, play, short story, or original story idea), research materials, variant drafts of scripts (from story outline to treatment to shooting script), post-production items such as press books and dialogue continuities, and legal records (details of the acquisition of the property, copyright registration, and contracts with actors and directors). Editors of the Wisconsin/Warner Bros. Screenplay Series receive copies of all the materials, along with prints of the films (the most authoritative ones available for reference purposes), to use in preparing the introductions and annotating the final shooting scripts.

In the process of preparing the screenplays for publication, typographical errors were corrected, punctuation and capitalization were modernized, and the format was redesigned to facilitate readability.

Unless otherwise specified, the photographs are frame enlargements taken from a 35-mm print of the film provided by United Artists.

In 1977 Warner Brothers donated the company's production records and distribution records to the University of Southern California and Princeton University, respectively. These materials are now available to researchers and complement the contents of the Warner Film Library donated to the Center by United Artists.

Tino Balio
General Editor

Acknowledgments

For granting me the opportunity to edit this volume, I am grateful to Tino Balio, director of the Wisconsin Center for Film and Theater Research. He and his staff also provided facilities conducive to research and writing at Madison during the summer of 1978. I also wish to thank the Motion Picture Association of America in Beverly Hills, California, for granting me access to its files of the censorship history of the film.

I especially wish to thank John Bright for generously sharing with me his recollections and a bit of the spirit of the time in an interview in January 1978. George Sochan and Michael Sylvia assisted in the chores of frame shot selection, research, and continuity editing, and Sylvia Rdzak ably prepared the typescript of the continuity notes.

I had always greatly enjoyed *The Public Enemy*; yet, undertaking to analyze systematically why this was so has involved me in many surprises. For those I accept full responsibility.

H. C.

Introduction: *An Ordinary Thug*

Henry Cohen

The beginning of the film *The Public Enemy* was a sprawling, unruly draft of a coauthored novel. In three hundred single-spaced pages of "Beer and Blood," John Bright and Kubec Glasmon drew upon the public history and their own knowledge and experiences of Chicago in the 1920s to construct a story in which verisimilitude was achieved partly by adapting actual incidents and characters.

Bright, born in 1908, and Glasmon, ten years older, had grown up in Chicago. During his high school years, Bright recounts, he worked as a "soda jerk" and delivery boy in Glasmon's drugstore and soda fountain, and it was there that the two young men became directly acquainted with Chicago gangsters. An important part of the business was the sale and delivery of the alcoholic beverages outlawed under national Prohibition from 1920 to 1933. Glasmon, trained as a pharmacist, first owned a store on the far North Side of the city, on Granville Street about two blocks from Lake Michigan. There, not far from where Bright grew up, the future writers got to know some of the flourishing gangsters in their clientele, Irish, Jewish, and others. They also became acquainted with some of the rising Italian gangsters, especially after Glasmon sold his store and bought one in the "badlands" of the South Side at Fifty-fourth Street and Cottage Grove Avenue.

"I worshipped those guys," Bright recalled. He and Glasmon were sometimes taken along in their nightclubbing, and they quickly learned to enjoy the clubs on their own. They witnessed the spectacle of one of Al Capone's explosive rages, joining the rest of the bystanders in prudently clearing out of the place. But chiefly the gangsters they came to know were the Irish, who were being largely supplanted, and those of East European heritage.

Bright, who had worked one summer as a copy boy on William Randolph Hearst's *Chicago American* in the days of Ben Hecht, aspired to be a writer; Chicago was his raw material. Glasmon, believing in his young friend, supported him as he wrote his first book, a popular biography of Chicago's most notorious mayor, the gangland-linked "Big Bill" Thompson. The drugstore financed them, being abandoned by way of an insurance fire, and the two friends went to New York where they found a publisher for the book in 1930. Then Bright decided to follow a girl to California and they departed by boat via the Panama Canal, spending most of their funds at the ports of call en route. They had barely enough left to rent a cottage on the outskirts of Hollywood, having decided on "Beer and Blood" as their next, and joint, writing venture.

Wondering how they would support themselves during the writing, Bright and Glasmon had scarcely begun when two Chicago acquaintances drove up. They were racketeer brothers, old patrons of the drugstore, who needed a business address and would pay the budding writers six months' expenses for the use of theirs. Bright and Glasmon graciously accommodated these dei ex machina. The wolf repelled from the door, they happily returned to the typewriter.

The logical place to market the story was Warner Brothers. A reforming, or at least "muckraking," relevance to contemporary life was the announced new company doctrine. Story ideas would be found in the newspaper headlines. Realism was to be emphasized (although the final products would contain plenty of sentimentality). Implicitly, the puffery suggested that a fast-paced, tough-talking portrayal of society would be more responsible than the naive and genteel popular romanticism that had dominated the silent screen. Americans, in the second year of their worst economic depression, would enjoy a vicarious participation in "real" life, not merely following and approving the action, but as critics. This orientation would tend to replace a sentimental poeticism with a contemporary, sound-enhanced momentum; movies could be made more cheaply and quickly, and be more entertaining in the bargain.

Warner Brothers had already launched a new gangster movie cycle with *Doorway to Hell* and *Little Caesar*. Laboring under the typical American compulsion for something "new," Warner's production chief, Darryl Zanuck, wondered whether the two successes had saturated the market. Nevertheless, he heard what he wanted to hear when William Wellman, striving for the directing assignment, assured him that he would make the movie (according to slightly varying recollections) "the toughest," "the most vicious," "the most realistic" gangster movie yet.

Warner Brothers purchased the motion picture rights to "Beer and Blood" for twenty-eight hundred dollars on December 1, 1930. Bright and Glasmon were also given seven-year contracts as screenwriters. (Their salaries were to escalate to four hundred dollars a week by the end of the contract.) But in view of their inexperience, the screenplay adaptation of the novel was assigned to Harvey Thew. (Bright and Glasmon shortly turned out the next three movies, after his first leading role in *Public Enemy*, that James Cagney would appear in: *Smart Money, Blonde Crazy,* and *Taxi*.) Warner Brothers also purchased the novelization rights to the screenplay, which it sold to Grosset and Dunlap for four hundred dollars down on March 2, 1931. By January 22 the title *The Public Enemy* had been adopted for the film, but there was a rumor out of New York that a wholly unrelated book by that title was nearing publication; Bright and Glasmon's manuscript was doctored by an anonymous flack hired by the studio and rushed into print in a cheap edition by March 20 to establish the copyright. (The few illustrations were posed publicity stills and the writing was so emasculated that Bright threw away his copies.) The book sold seventeen thousand copies (there would have been royalties only after fifty thousand) and was out of print in a year and a half. Meanwhile, the movie was completed from a shooting script that had been prepared in a matter of weeks, apparently without preliminary drafts; if there were any, they have not survived.

Introduction

From Naturalism to Realism

"Beer and Blood," the source of both the published novel and the shooting script, has vitality and verisimilitude, and with its strengths it is easy to believe that the draft could have been hammered into an effective novel. Yet it has weaknesses too. It is virtually all incident and dialogue, with little that is descriptive, analytical, or expository. Some of the strengths were readily transmitted to the screenplay, and even enhanced. What is more, serious weaknesses and merely adequate writing were surmounted, or transmuted into effective moments in the script and its realization.

The draft novel lacks description. The Chicago settings, the neighborhoods, streets, restaurants, hotels, and so on are named but not described, nor are fictitious settings. People are characterized almost exclusively by speech and actions, not by physical traits.

On the other hand, the social environment is carefully indicated in structure and in some detail. Juvenile and adult gangs, their territories and ethnic identities; the gaudy tavern and club life; corruption in trade unions; the business organization and economics of the illegal liquor business and its internal problems; the pervasive corruption of politics and the law—these are delineated concisely and vigorously.

For Bright and Glasmon, what was central was personal encounter in dialogue and incident. Their style reflected, in a way, the modern urban reality, where such encounters occur much more frequently than they do in rural areas. There was comparatively little reflective narrative. Even analysis was usually conveyed in the form of one character's explanation to another in the dialogue. These first-person presentations, often vivid, envelop the reader with a greater sense of presence than the usual exposition.

The psychological meaning of the transmutation from novel to film has a more traditional formulation: a naturalistic novel was made into a realistic movie.

In naturalism the "givens," primarily a bitterly competitive human environment created by biological and social inheri-

14

tance, are treated as deterministic of character, plot, and out-
come by a ruthless and seemingly unalterable logic. Literary
naturalism is pronouncedly Social Darwinian (the etymology is
suggestive), and while Darwinian natural selection and evolu-
tion "explain" change in nature, the immense time span of ev-
olutionary nature is irrelevant to human lives. Naturalistic au-
thors may sometimes have been, in their politics, reformers,
even revolutionaries, who sympathized with victims and sought
to alter the outcomes of social processes by altering the social
environment; but in their work, environment (like the moment)
was fixed, and within it the flexibility of the human character
was severely limited and outcomes were "predetermined" to
the point of fatalism. Driven with remorseless logic by the given
nature of circumstances and humanity, characters tended to become, and to be at the mercy of, driven personalities much like
those that were becoming, in the same era that saw the full
flowering of literary naturalism, the subjects of Freudian psychology. The protagonists of naturalistic fiction were as incapable of conscious self-direction as the disturbed patients of the
pioneer psychoanalysts. In their driven states of mind there was
little possibility of humor, except for the derisive kinds. And
they were as incapable of effective choice. Powerless playthings
of society and nature, they could not be effectively responsible.
Guilt, heroism, tragedy, tended (with rare exceptions) to become irrelevant, most explicitly in the works of those writers
who considered themselves "scientific."

A trend like naturalism does not simply grow out of the history or psychology of its time; it is a part of them, as they are a
part of it. Naturalism has realistic validity as an approach to or
expression of extreme psychological states, or situations to
which they may be relevant; but, as with any other mode, its
choice entails sacrifices in return for its gains. Gangster life
would seem to be as suitable as any phenomena for a naturalistic approach; yet, for all the human monsters there are among
gangsters, the pseudo-classics of the genre are merely mystify-
ing when they are devoid of organic individual or social
growth—when they lose realism, taken as accuracy of percep-
tion, description, and explanation.

There was some of the two-dimensional in the naturalism of "Beer and Blood," from its beginnings with a brutal battle of children, very reminiscent of the opening of Stephen Crane's *Maggie: A Girl of the Streets*, to its hyperclimactic ending. Yet, given the nature of many criminals, even a highly colored naturalism, provided it did not lose touch with the organic life of the society, could be at the same time realistic. The revisions, through script to film, cumulatively diminishing the pathological and strengthening the ordinary elements in characterization and plot, resulted in a realistic movie. "Beer and Blood" has a relentless, almost mechanistic determinism and sometimes derisive tone (e.g., Mrs. Powers is described as looking like a "sack of potatoes"). But the film has James Cagney's Tom groping unconsciously and inarticulately toward a greater awareness of self and others, as in the serious portions of his scenes (which we may not find completely convincing in themselves) with Gwen and in the reconciliation with his brother, after he has learned that he too is vulnerable. He has learned to choose—too late. He might have become a more genuinely human person, someone like—well, like the real-life Cagney. His death has been invested with something of the tragic.

The sharp and accurate language was basic to the realism. Gangster speech was saturated with obscenities that could not be used publicly in that era, and the slang had to carry the burden of authenticity and to thrill an audience still somewhat traditionally inhibited but highly responsive to novelty and color. (This was not original, of course; *Little Caesar*, from the novel by W. R. Burnett, and other books and films had made use of gangster lingo, though seldom before so richly or authentically.) In twentieth-century theater and film (and in nineteenth-century publishing) the new urban and gangster styles and stories had long proven their popularity.

The characters of the novel, and their names, were of four kinds of derivations:

1. Some were wholly fictional, or so obscure or generalized that specific life models are indistinguishable: Tom Powers, Matt Doyle, Paddy Ryan, Putty Nose, the women, and so on.

2. Many real characters (Al Capone and others) appear in

passing, or to populate the background; their names come up in conversation and anecdote. This category was dropped from the film, lessening verisimilitude but generalizing the setting so that it might seem to be, perhaps, any sizable American city. (Perhaps it was decided, too, not to take even remote chances of libel suits. After the film had opened, the name of the Congress Hotel was removed from one of the scenes when the respectable Chicago hostelry of that name politely implied the threat of a lawsuit.)

3. One character was drawn directly from life with only the last name altered: Nails Nathan was copied from Samuel "Nails" Morton.

4. Reality and fiction were blurred by fusing known and unique first names with fictitious last names or wholly fictitious characters: Schemer Burns is reminiscent of Schemer Drucci in name, though not otherwise, and Don O'Brien of Dion O'Banion. This group, too, was eliminated in the script, leaving only the first category and Nails Nathan.

These variations occur in incidents too. Most are fictitious. The death of Nails Nathan, however, was exactly that of Nails Morton; the latter's outraged associates really did execute the guilty horse. The famous scene in which Tom mashes the grapefruit in his girlfriend's face is drawn from Chicago lore, which told of Hymie Weiss doing it with an omelet. (The ambush in which Matt is killed, which does not occur in "Beer and Blood," resembles the one in which Weiss died.) The novel's references to gangs also use these techniques, with one instance of ambiguity. The Druggan-Lake gang is mentioned as if it had no connection with Tom and Matt, who were actually inspired by its two leaders—but with a mixture of resemblances and dissimilarities. (In the novel, Tom emulates Terry Druggan when he reaches through the bars of his cell, seizes a contemptuous reporter by the collar, and brutally jerks his face repeatedly into the bars.) Youth gangs, typical of those that linked juveniles and adults (somewhat as the Red Oaks Club does), cross the pages: the Hamburgers, the Ragen Colts, the Hogen Colts. The result of these adaptations of reality is one of the most developed of the journalistic novels, that half-literature that has become so common on modern best-seller lists. This one, for all its flaws in first draft, remains superior to most of its kind.

Changes in Characters and Structure

At the first story conference Zanuck said to the young writers that "Beer and Blood" told "five stories"; the film would have to concentrate on one. The decision to make it the story of Tom Powers as a sort of rake's progress, reflected in the new title, *The Public Enemy*, was understandable, given the current ruling assumption that it had to fit into one half of a double bill, but it meant sacrificing much of value. It led not only to draining much of the reportorial richness from the story, but also to the simplification of characterization, relationships, and plot. All that survives in the shooting script of the social detail (with the important but brief exceptions of Tom's domestic environment and Putty Nose's club) is a moment's picturization of the coming of Prohibition, a mention by Paddy Ryan of his "influence," a shot of a policeman enjoying his illegal beer, a few other implicating glimpses. There is some dramatic justification for the sacrifice in the intensified concentration on Tom Powers, but much is lost in the shift of emphasis from the social, and the socially critical, to the individual. It tends partly to vitiate the exaggerated references, in writing about American movies, to the superior social consciousness of Warner Brothers. The studio usually pulled its punches before they could land at any vital point. The pity is that there would have been plenty of time for some of the human setting of Tom Powers's life story with no sacrifice of camera and dialogue pace, yet even what little survived in the shooting script of Bright and Glasmon's depiction of the society was trimmed. Except for some touches that were undoubtedly perceived simply as color, but in reality—thanks to Wellman's and Devereaux Jennings's pictorial brilliance—were more than that, almost everything after the opening scenes was a simple personal history, which was presumed to be what the audience wanted.

Some of the slang was retained from "Beer and Blood," or at any rate enough for flavor (though some of it would be cut out of the film by local censors); but much also was lost in the transfer. This type of color (from chapter 25 of "Beer and Blood") did not survive in the film: "'Where does the Polak get the Burns monicker?' Tom asked. 'Where do any of 'em get 'em?' Gordon responded. 'Jack McGurn's a wop, Bugs Moran and Hymie Weiss are Polaks, Jimmy Wells is a Jew, Al [Capone] Brown's a dago—Hell, a name ain't no indication o' what a guy is.'" Except for the apparently Jewish name of Nails Nathan, virtually all reference to ethnic groups other than Irish was eliminated. (But the Italians, of course, had just gotten the treatment in the likes of *Little Caesar* and *Doorway to Hell*.)

The cumulative result of the many changes from "Beer and Blood" is a story and a protagonist classic in their very ordinariness. Tom's values and vices—his craving for excitement, money, and glamour, his ruthlessness and violence in their pursuit (but not without limit even in the novel, where he considers himself above the indignity of the pimp, who profits off women), his average mind—all his qualities combine to make a classically ordinary criminal. He is clearly a disordered, not a healthy personality; but he is far from the fixed, two-dimensional flatness and the extreme, pathological mental states that are contrived for us out of no particular environment, out of generalized thin air, in the forms of Rico, Tony Camonte, Cody in other movies of the gangster genre: *Little Caesar*, *Scarface*, *White Heat*.

Changing the portrayal of Tom, reducing the pathological, monstrous characteristics of his original version to the proportions of a more ordinary personality, meant changing the story. In an episode in "Beer and Blood," the young brother of his abandoned girlfriend, a harmless noncriminal, timidly seeks out the prosperous Tom to ask him to finance an abortion of the pregnancy he had left her with. In an explosion of hate Tom attacks and stomps the mild-mannered lad with such ferocity that he suffers facial fractures and has to be taken to the hospital; even Tom's criminal associates are shocked and appalled. Nothing like such uncontrolled rage appears in the script or the film. Rage may be latent, even clearly so, but the violence that is at the ready is only let loose in reasonable proportion to the provocation or the necessity. Moreover, victims, too, are assigned a share of responsibility: the policeman shot and killed by Tom and Matt had first opened fire on them and killed their partner; cowardice is imputed to the saloonkeeper who is slapped into buying the gang's beer.

Tom Powers has the virtue of loyalty to his friends; in fact, his loyalty helps drive him to his end. This virtue is carried over from the original, and even enhanced, although with some complications. One of the most unfortunate cuts, compelled by the censors and perpetuated in the prints that remain in general use, obscures the reason for his violent disgust with Jane after she seduces him. Because of the objections to showing illicit sexual relations with anything but disapproval, if at all, the movie as commonly seen leaves it unclear that Jane is Paddy's mistress. Partly for this reason, many writers have misinterpreted as simply misogyny Tom's disgust that, however stupefied by drink, he has betrayed in the worst imaginable way the man who is his patron, benefactor, and friend (and implicitly, perhaps, his adoptive father-figure).

It is in his flight from this situation, in the movie (unlike the novel, in which Matt's death occurs after Tom's disappearance), that his boyhood friend is gunned down in ambush. From this traumatic chain of events he rushes to Gwen's apartment, only to discover that she has left (in impact, betrayed) him. In the novel, it is only the sexual betrayals, and not Matt's death— which occurs later—that impel Tom in disgust and rage on his final errand. The added motivation, in the movie, of Matt's death enhances the sense of male loyalty in a way that is compatible with intelligent plotting and characterization, but in so doing vitiates the other outrages upon his virtue.

The decision to simplify the structure of *The Public Enemy* by making it the biography of Tom Powers also resulted in the reworking of the characters closest to him, and further contributed to the transformation of "Beer and Blood" from a naturalistic novel into a realistic movie.

Matt, in "Beer and Blood," is not quite the simple foil that he remains throughout the film. He is the lesser figure, the follower from boyhood on, but he has a greater degree of toughness and independence, and he gradually becomes more self-assertive, sometimes even clashing with Tom. The joke Tom repeats when he is with him in *Public Enemy*, that Matt has company but he is alone, would not do for the character who shows flashes of restiveness and irritation under his partner's harsh, domineering, hypersensitive, and humorless outbursts. In the reading the suspicion grows that without the outside pressures holding them together to the denouement, the two old friends might have parted, perhaps even ended as enemies. Not that characters such as the movie Matt are unreal: they are known, among gangsters too, and Matt the passive follower in his relationship with Tom is validly a tough partner toward the rest of the world. Still, the novel was much more true to life, especially given the notorious fragility of gangster friendships.

Mike remains the heir to their father's authority and their mother's gentility, so exacerbating to his relationship with Tom; but the plot and character changes involving him are also important. In "Beer and Blood" the rest of the gang, including Matt, try to rescue his kidnapped brother, or his corpse. Mike, his family loyalty suddenly asserting itself, reverts to a wartime frenzy, seizes his souvenir hand grenades, and joins the gang in a raid on the enemy. They capture an inept rear guard, but threats and beatings elicit no information before the captives are executed. As the gang departs, the furious Mike, not realizing that Matt is still inside, hurls a grenade into the building, killing him. Only back at the Powers home, after Mike's rage is spent, does Paddy tell him of this final homicidal irony. While the depleted Mike slumps under the news, he is summoned by the ring of the doorbell and Tom's body falls in upon him, bringing "Beer and Blood" to its end.

In general the "secondary" characters (in terms of time on screen) that survived into the screenplay are consistent with the originals of "Beer and Blood." Ma Powers, Putty Nose, Paddy Ryan, Nails Nathan, Mamie, Katy, and the briefer parts are accurate versions although condensed. But a few of the ancillary roles, like the major ones, are altered: they are still recognizable, yet they become significantly different beings, and the ensuing slight changes of plot (with the mutations of character) help give the movie a different tone.

In both the novel and the shooting script Gwen is an adventuress, but she has other nuances in "Beer and Blood." She cannot live with Tom because if she were found out her suit for divorce might be jeopardized. Tom (and his milieu) interests, even attracts her, although this is no grand passion; but she leaves him, not simply out of pique because she cannot control him, but because she will not risk her freedom and because she is induced to renew an old school friendship, one that is also lesbian. In both versions her departure adds to Tom's rage and helps bring on his attack upon the rival gang, but in the novel it is, comparatively, a somewhat more important motive than in the screenplay. Still, if a bit less exotic in its final version, the filmed role does not have a drastically different impact upon Tom or the plot.

Tom's policeman father, whose appearance at the beginning of the movie is important beyond its wordless brevity, is a more amply if conventionally developed presence in the opening chapters of "Beer and Blood." He is also, in one way, a more perverse presence: he does not beat Tom for fighting, but for losing the fight! There is an added irony in his death (which is unexplained in the script), considering his younger son's future career, for he is killed in the line of duty by a criminal. In the movie he is a much more remote authority figure, and psychologically much more effective.

On the Set

Bright and Glasmon had met the young, famous "Wild Bill" Wellman at the Warner Brothers cafeteria. Fascinated by their tales of Chicago gangsters, he asked to see "Beer and Blood" and then with their concurrence went after the assignment. Zanuck, it appears, at first planned to use Archie Mayo, who had just directed one of the studio's emerging line of gangster films, *Doorway to Hell*. Mayo, however, did not want the job for fear of being stereotyped as a gangster-movie director. He went happily off to make a "woman's movie," providing the opportunity.

Wellman's abilities and personality attracted Zanuck. The producer cultivated toughness, working hard at athletics and the outdoor life. Wellman, with his history of heroics and deviltry, fascinated him, and perhaps awed him a little. Quarterback of his high school football team, hockey player, wounded pilot-hero of World War I, motorcyclist, hard-drinking womanizer, this genuine article seemed a flattering complement to Zanuck, who selected him as a rare companion on elaborate hunting expeditions to distant wilds. Their relationship does not seem ever to have been quite perfectly relaxed, but the two men cultivated each other. In 1930 Wellman made his first two movies for Zanuck, *Maybe It's Love*, a negligible "Joe College" comedy distinguished only by a seemingly innocuous but bawdily suggestive dance scene, and *Other Men's Women* (also known as *Steel Highway*), a melodrama with some odd twists and strong acting and direction. Zanuck picked Wellman for *Public Enemy*, and, for the first time at Warner Brothers, the director threw himself into a film with a personal sense of discovery and enthusiasm.

Wellman has been underrated as a director. He directed many potboilers but so did all the others in the business: it was the price they paid for the occasional opportunity to do something worthwhile. Wellman, like all other honest craftsmen, was frank about it. To him the script, together with the director, were the sine qua non of a good movie. The bad scripts he would turn into films with maximum assembly line efficiency; when the script had possibilities he would try to bring them out. He had proven he could mount a grand, and expensive, spectacle with his famous production of *Wings* at Paramount, winner of the first Academy Award in 1929, but he was also proud of his workmanlike ability to bring productions in with quality, under budget, and within schedules. His economy of means and of dollars commanded one of the highest salaries on the market at about $150,000 per year, and apparently more than usual influence in casting (although subject to Zanuck's last word). Shooting began in February 1931. Wellman finished *Public Enemy* in twenty-six days and well under budget, he told Cagney, for $151,000, which was low for a feature film even by Depression standards.

Wellman's touch stands out in any comparison of *The Public*

Enemy with other films of the genre. Comparison with the shooting script is even more revealing. Often he seems to be competently following the script; but at times he follows it, and sometimes departs from it, with originality, even brilliance. (It appears, circumstantially, that cameraman Devereaux Jennings was on the whole simply the executor of Wellman's vision, although this cannot be directly confirmed. Jennings was one of the leading Warner Brothers technicians in the early 1930s, shooting about half of the studio's early technicolor productions, but there is almost no biographical data on him.)

The very first shot, beginning to establish the milieu, departs from the glamourous, expansive lakeshore skyline cliché called for in the script and gives us instead the closed-in, crowded, grayish downtown Chicago Loop. The early moments (from stock footage) set the rapid pace of much of the movie (and the sound too, like the later staccato of gunfire, and of Cagney's speech) by quick cuts and by emphasis on semidiagonal perspective lines and motion. Much more interesting, however, are the ways Wellman visually develops certain themes (see Illustrations).

A tense triad is formed of Tom, authority, and the camera. With insight and efficiency the camera portrays an emotionally remote and brutal father who looms impersonal and hostile, a force to be evaded, outwitted, endured, and somehow (subconsciously) overcome. The camera looking up with Tom at his father suggests the earlier sequence of Tom and Matt looking back up the department store escalator, as if to trace the latter situation to its roots in the former. From these beginnings, the camera does not belittle Tom. It sometimes looks at him from a realistic eye-level vantage point; but often it looks up at him, sometimes subtly, sometimes emphatically, elevating and exalting him, as if enacting his own subconscious. The camera angle that is so commonly used as a means of subjugating the audience to whatever the screen is doing is here, for once, psychologically right. The return, at the last, to or beyond the extreme upward-looking angles of Tom's childhood is not only the correct technical means to maximum shock; it carries its own psychological and dramatic irony.

Wellman uses near-pantomime to enact some of the crucial relationships. The awkward counterpoint of the brothers contrasts with the balletic harmony of Tom and the devoted Matt, so suggestive, in placement and gesture (and words), of psychological "twinning." Matt's moment of death, too, pantomimes an irony: his end as Tom's unwitting shield is fitting to his life as his emotional foil. The balletic harmony ends in a (for once) writhing agony of death.

Wellman also enhances the script by cataloguing the little everyday defiances of a just-urbanized "lower" class toward middle-class manners: obscenity, the pool room, spitting, hard liquor and beer, contempt for education and patriotism, the boor of the breakfast table. Vulgarity invades the very bastion of the outraged, bewildered, genteel home. The family reunion dinner, dominated by the beer keg in the middle of the table as by some strange alien idol, is a great comic shot.

Most bemusing of all, perhaps, is the transformation of Tom's ironic near-seduction by Gwen when Wellman infuses into that scene his own special sardonic glee. Taken at script value, Tom softens as never before. As a stage, or even a destination, of a stormy maturation, this would not be absolutely impossible for our no longer naturalistic protagonist, especially given this fleshy, well-built, hard-to-get blonde. Still, her dialogue is stagey, and with the soggy background music of the sort that was to become an epidemic disease of movies intruding in this one for the first and almost the only time, probably any other director of the day would have given us the kind of standard sappiness that divides audiences into wallowing sentimentalists and sardonic realists.

What happens on Wellman's screen is something else. Jean Harlow was one of the last beauties in a nearly completed transition. After centuries, an ideal of women whose voluptuousness overflowed from compact bodies and short limbs, domestic and maternal whatever the lady's metier, was being usurped by the taller, slimmer-waisted, more agile woman. But here we find the pleasures of cultural lag: appropriately dressed and coiffed, Harlow, built more like a future Ma Powers than, say, a Joan Crawford, is posed on a chaise longue as if for a painting by David instead of a Hollywood camera. The dame with the midwestern accent who had talked of coming from Texas seems utterly unconcerned with that nervous character in the background, hat askew and cleaning his nails as, brow furrowed, he gropes for articulation. As if the scene were not visually and aurally fragmented enough, the mind is hard put to concentrate on any of it because the eye is being subverted, drawn away insidiously by that zany statuette (see figure 30). (Wellman threw something like it into a melodramatic scene in his earlier *Other Men's Women.*) With these accompaniments even Gwen's little speech and the sentimental music almost become ironic, part of the act of a moderately crafty provincial charmer, a kind of Mae West played straight. (It might not even be too much to hear the soppy music, for once, as the expression of *his* state of mind.) If that terminal false moment, the hackneyed throwing-the-glass-in-the-fireplace bit, is cut, perhaps in favor of a shrug of the shoulders, Wellman's scene could stand with the great moments of Hollywood comedies.

The most famous scene in the movie—Tom mashing the half grapefruit in Kitty's face—was an instantaneous, overwhelming success. Cagney's own words are the most apt description: "It was just about the first time, if not the very first, that a woman had been treated like a broad on the screen, instead of like a delicate flower." And yet, unfortunately, it is not quite that simple. There were mini-masochistic and mini-sadistic thrills for some of the audience, certainly, along with surprise and shock, and perhaps far more of delight at the novel honesty of the moment, an honesty as liberating to women as to men. But, while Tom treats Kitty like a broad, the code-influenced script and movie, in one of the few false moments, treat her like a delicate flower.

The right ending to the scene would have been more like Bright and Glasmon's, in which Kitty grabs the first thing available, a glass of water, and douses Tom with it; or more like the real ending at the studio, after the cameras stopped. Actress Mae Clarke, suffering from a severe cold, had been assured that the scene would be faked and the illusion of a half grapefruit being mashed in her face would be achieved by camera angle.

Wellman, however, characteristically took Cagney aside and in-
sisted that the scene must be real, that Clarke's unpreparedness
would guarantee an honest shot, that it would make him a star.
The gentlemanly Cagney, who off-screen would never have in-
flicted such an assault, least of all on a woman, was reluctant,
but finally yielded to Wellman's gleeful urgings. At the end of
the day Hollywood people, ever quick to seize the occasion,
adjourned to strange parties to pray alcoholically to their gods—
Christian, Jewish, voodoo—that the single take would emerge
intact from the lab, for it was doubtful that they would be able
to get Clarke back for a retake. Clarke had stormed up and
down the set denouncing all and sundry in explicit language—
Cagney ("You Irish . . . "), Wellman, cast, crew, studio—and
then departed, never (for the moment, anyway) to return. (She
ultimately relented: if the scene did not exactly make her a star,
it did keep her in demand for years, for punching-bag roles.)

The original ending of the screenplay apparently was not
filmed, the code office having suggested that this outburst by
the returned war hero added excessive violence and should be
deleted. (The truncated final scene, with Mike stalking too pon-
derously from his brother's corpse, looks as if the original ending of the script had been filmed, but apparently reflects the
hurried decision, within two weeks of production, to simply cut
the conclusion off at that point.) The clumsy ending of the
movie, with Mike's vestigial stagger and the winding down of
the phonograph record, remains as mere punctuation, a hurried
period to the whole. It might better have ended with the delivery of Tom's body and Mike looking up toward where their
mother is singing, with sentimentality, irony, and tragedy all in
balance.

The casting had much to do with how well it all worked.
James Cagney is almost infinitely varied in expression, and always just right; to study him frame by frame can only expand
and deepen our admiration for his embodiment of Tom Powers.
Fully effective in communicating the violence and suggesting
an underlying rage, he is equally so in showing fear, and the
engaging if limited flashes of humor that the original novel and
the script in cold type did not convey.

It is one of the best-known bits of Hollywood lore that it almost never happened. At first, Edward Woods had been cast as Tom, Cagney as Matt. Wellman, typically for those days, was still finishing another job when shooting began on *The Public Enemy*, and not for several days did he catch up with the rushes. By then Bright and Glasmon were after him to reverse the Cagney and Woods assignments. Wellman saw and agreed, and asked Zanuck to approve the switch. Zanuck was hesitant, pointing out that Woods was engaged to the daughter of Louella O. Parsons, gossip columnist of the Hearst newspaper chain and, as such, one of the more preposterous factors in the industry of that era. Again, Wellman's rejoinder was the right one for its target: "Well, are you going to let some newspaperwoman run your business?" The switch was made. (It was a bitter disappointment to Woods, who never again came so close to a starring role. He would get favorable reviews in a few supporting roles during the next few years before retiring to live on real estate investments. He could never have approached Cagney's performance, any more than could anyone else, but he was excellent as Tom's rewritten, psychologically diminished "twin.")

The other male characterizations in general are almost perfect, down to the walk-ons who ornament the Red Oaks Club. Donald Cook is almost too overwrought as Tom's brother. London-born Murray Kinnell is a Dickensian fagin. Robert Emmett O'Connor, born in Milwaukee, seems bred to the role of an Irish-American tavern statesman. Leslie Fenton is ideal as Nails Nathan. In that character Bright and Glasmon modeled a kind of Jewish Gatsby, a soldier of fortune risen from Maxwell Street, earthy and urbane, street-wise and cosmopolitan, colorful and stylish. Most of his authentic conversation in the novel is lost; yet Fenton communicates more of him—and the hardness too—than could have been expected. This Gatsby is vigorously alive, not the dreamy, yearning, almost fairy-tale gangster of Fitzgerald's famous romance.

The most problematic casting is of several of the women. The briefer roles are professionally done, and Joan Blondell, her usual vivacious self, also captures for a moment the precisely right mixture of loyalty to Matt's best friend with fear and distaste for the implicit violence, the contemptuousness toward women, the uncontrollable danger that Tom carries. A fine actress, Blondell was delightfully easy to take. Not so, for many, Beryl Mercer and Jean Harlow in their roles.

More than any other, the role of Tom's mother carries the heavy weight of her historical type. She personifies all the idealized sweetly harmonious domesticity of the late nineteenth-century doll's house from which the determinedly masculine fled to the clubs and taverns. Beryl Mercer's acting is not sentimental; the role is. It portrays a reality, one that was still dominant when the older characters in the movie would have been young, when the older viewers in the audience had been young, a reality still surviving in the inevitable time lag of cultural change.

Jean Harlow, always a crowd pleaser, displeased some critics, in this and other roles, with her limited acting abilities, but as Gwen she is right. Gwen is not a "hooker," nor a sophisticated society girl, as several critics have called her. Gwen displays experience and savvy, but hers is still a limited sophistication well within her actress's range and style. Harlow's Gwen can convincingly manipulate Tom, but still is in his league.

The Problem of Censorship

Movie producers were increasingly dismayed by the threatened costly proliferation of controversy and legal actions in scores of censorship jurisdictions, state and local, governmental or self-appointed, at home and abroad, under varying laws and standards. The production code, and its administrative office, had been designed in 1930 (following earlier inadequate beginnings) for a purpose much like that which American governmental regulatory agencies have commonly served: to act as a buffer between harassed producers and the often critical but fragmented public, offering a measure of compromise in hopes of retaining a measure of freedom. As such, the code office still favored freedom of film action more than would later be the case. *The Public Enemy* exemplified this, but also added to the controversy that by 1934 would push the boundaries of the permissible some distance back upon the moviemakers.

Despite official precautions, but in keeping with the real hopes of those who made the movie, the realism of much of what emerged on the screen was startling, even shocking. Some of it, to conservative moralists on the defensive in a chronically turbulent society stricken by the Great Depression, tended to subvert "American" (that is, middle-class) values and institutions. The movie seemed to show that crime and violence did pay, at least before the end, in money, glamour, thrills, women; and that the police and the law were ineffectual or irrelevant, for even when criminals were threatened and retribution exacted it was only by other criminals. It gave tactical lessons in crime: how to mount an ambush with machine guns, for example. It displayed deviance, briefly, in the shape of a "pansy" tailor. (Despite misgivings among previewers, there were no public outcries against this scene. The insinuation of effeminacy in expensive, high-fashion men's clothing was typical of Hollywood ambivalence, although this case was rather more gross than most.) It offended against the sanctity of the family in showing Tom and Kitty living together out of wedlock.

Probably, too, the film's implicit attack upon Prohibition as a major cause of the swollen gangster violence and wealth of the twenties rankled many provincial Americans who were still defending that ill-fated reform against the repeal that would come in 1933. This was not a point made explicitly by critics of *The Public Enemy*, but many of the attacks came from centers of Prohibition sentiment. These tended to be (though by no means exclusively) in Protestant rural and small town America, to which the entire "new" immigrant, urban, "wet" society was alien.

It was easy enough, in those days, to foresee objections, and there were some efforts to forestall them. En route to its approval of the script and the film, the code office solicited the opinion of August Vollmer, the reform-minded Berkeley, California, police chief who was then the best-known spokesman for a higher "professionalism" within his occupation. Vollmer upheld the anticriminal morality of the portrayal of Tom

Powers's rise and fall. He was, however, something of a rarity, one of the most cosmopolitan and forward looking of police officials. More representative were the New York City officials who resented the innocuousness of their screen counterparts.

There was a difficult problem to anticipate: the many public or self-constituted censors. The studio attempted to forestall their attacks, and threats of damaging boycotts, cuts, or license denials, by a measure of self-censorship. For example, when Nails Morton of Chicago had been thrown from his horse and killed, his loyal confrères escorted the animal to the scene of the mishap in Lincoln Park, where they shot it dead before the astonished stares of picnickers and passersby. Entertaining as such a spectacle might have been to movie audiences, the hostility of the American Society for the Prevention of Cruelty to Animals to any such public display of cruelty was not to be aroused by prudent businessmen. Thus the execution was heard off-screen, but not seen. Even cruelty to humans on-screen was under attack, and the shooting of Putty Nose and Tom's vengeance upon the enemy after Matt's death also are heard without being seen.

Was this off-screen technique used on its own merits because it would enlist the active imagination of the spectator, or in deference to the "Production Code" of the motion picture trade association? The first interpretation is not unthinkable, but probably a creative adaptation to industry self-censorship is the true explanation. Before shooting began the script was voluntarily submitted to the self-censorship code unit within the Hays Office. (The Motion Picture Producers and Distributors of America was so known, informally, during the long presidency of Will Hays. Later in 1931 script submission in advance was made mandatory for all members.) There was little, it was hoped, that need provoke attack in the way of sex or language, the obscenities and ethnic slurs having been excised. What violence would remain on-screen was not gratuitous or glorified; the adaptation and filming of the draft novel successfully avoided many of its obvious pitfalls. (Did the widespread fears that crime movies were teaching techniques to potential criminals, for example, cause one of the false moments in the movie when Tom, acquiring a fresh supply of handguns, asks to see "the big one—the .38"? The phrase makes no sense, and indeed the script correctly identifies "the big one" as a .45 caliber weapon. Or was this merely an uncharacteristic slip of the tongue, overlooked or deemed not worth the trouble of a retake?)

The advertising implied and contributed to these tensions, in a way that also reflected the rival pulls of naturalism and realism. So far as it had any substance, the pressbook—made up chiefly in the form of press releases and articles furnished whole for the general run of copy-starved, frugal, or interested newspaper editors—emphasized the realism of the movie, that is, its accuracy of plot, portrayal, and up-to-date language. As such, and in much of the writing, it tended to be factual, reasonably literate, and middle class in orientation. The publicity stills, on the other hand, tended to be naturalistic in their exaggeration, and their violence, of pose, gesture, and manner: glaring eyes, men with one arm around a girl and the other pointing a gun, stark silhouetting against blank backgrounds, with these effects still further heightened in the blown-up posters tinted in lurid shades—sensational enticements to the nonliterate and pre-adult in the mass audience.

Outside the United States, too, the movie met with hostility. Even in markets where Prohibition and ethnic strife could be dismissed as American aberrations, the gunplay and violence were objectionable. Cuts were demanded in such native locales as Wisconsin (where the denunciations were particularly vocal and well organized), Virginia, Ohio, and Baltimore, and in parts of the British Empire. The shooting of the horse (even off-screen), the return of Tom, dead, to his home, and other scenes were found (in different places) too horrid and disgusting for civilized viewers. Indeed, the outcries against this movie and others impelled the Hays Office to tighten industry self-censorship, and in 1935–36 *The Public Enemy* was denied approval for re-release (which compelled a fresh submission). Even as late as 1953, it was licensed for re-release only reluctantly, and after exacting the deletion of two lines that made clearer the illicit relationship of Paddy Ryan and his mistress. In Australia, and in Alberta, Canada, licensing was refused as late as 1951. In the

United Kingdom itself the British Film Board, after several cuts, classified the movie (retitled *Enemies of the Public*) "A," suitable for children only in the company of a parent or guardian, which cut off a sizable part of the market. Such sensitivities, undoubtedly, explain the surprisingly small foreign rentals earned, less than $93,000 in the years before World War II.

The reviews in the metropolitan press revealed little doubt in the reviewers' minds that Tom and his fellows were despicable. "Hoodlum" was the term usually applied; "unheroic," several termed him, although a few conceded that Tom had some attractive traits. One writer reviewed the audience. Thornton Delehanty of the *New York Post* was surprised that it laughed with and applauded Tom's feats; but, he reported with satisfaction, it was stunned into silence and left the theater crestfallen at his ending.

These varied and ambivalent responses were not simply the outcomes of different fixed viewpoints, like those from the audience for the shadows on the wall of Plato's cave. They resulted also from the evolving ambivalences of the transmuted "Beer and Blood," and of the historical culture.

The Public Enemy was one of the best American movies of 1931; yet the only Academy Award it received, or was nominated for, was that given to Bright and Glasmon for best original story. Cagney, admired as his acting was then and later, had to wait for his first Academy Award until 1942 for playing the patriotic songwriter George M. Cohan in *Yankee Doodle Dandy*. The unserious attitude toward *Public Enemy* seems to have been shared by its makers. Zanuck scandalized Wellman years later by claiming the credit for turning Mae Clarke's face into a grapefruit grinder, but except for the sensational and commercial aspects of their success those who made the movie took it hardly more seriously than the middle-class critics and public. Wellman and Cagney gave it little thought in their memoirs, and surviving author John Bright seems not to have considered it of much consequence. Yet it endures before today's audiences, not only as a fascinating document of its time but as a vital entertainment and work of film art.

SELECTED BIBLIOGRAPHY

Altman, Charles F. "Towards a History of American Film." *Cinema Journal*, Spring 1977.

Bright, John. *Hizzoner Big Bill Thompson: An Idyll of Chicago*. New York: Cape & Smith, 1930.

British Film Institute. *Monthly Film Bulletin* (1976).

Brooks, Louise. "On Location with Billy Wellman." *Film Culture*, Spring 1972.

Cagney, James. *Cagney by Cagney*. New York: Doubleday, 1976.

Campbell, Russell. "Warner Brothers in the Thirties." *Velvet Light Trap*, no. 1 (June 1971).

Clark, Norman H. *Deliver Us from Evil: An Interpretation of American Prohibition*. New York: Norton, 1976.

Fox, Julian. "A Man's World: An Analysis of the Films of William Wellman." *Films & Filming*, March–April 1973.

Gann, Ernest K. *A Hostage to Fortune*. New York: Knopf, 1978.

Gussow, Mel. *Don't Say Yes until I Finish Talking: A Biography of Darryl F. Zanuck*. New York: Doubleday, 1971.

Higham, Charles. *Warner Brothers*. New York: Scribners, 1975.

Jowett, Garth. "Bullets, Beer and the Hays Office: *Public Enemy* (1931)." In *American History/American Film*, edited by John E. O'Connor and Martin A. Jackson. New York: Ungar, 1979.

Kael, Pauline. "Raising Kane," *The Citizen Kane Book*. Boston: Little, Brown, 1971.

Kaminsky, Stuart. *American Film Genres*. Dayton: Pflaum, 1974.

Kobler, John. *Capone: The Life and World of Al Capone*. New York: Putnam, 1971.

Kohut, Heinz. *The Restoration of the Self*. New York: International Universities Press, 1977.

Macdonald, Dwight. *Dwight Macdonald on Movies*. Englewood Cliffs, N.J.: Prentice-Hall, 1969.

MacGovern, James R. "The American Woman's Pre-World War I Freedom in Manners and Morals." *Journal of American History*, September 1968.

Meyer, William R. *The Warner Brothers Directors*. New Rochelle, N.Y.: Arlington House, 1978.

Moley, Raymond. *The Hays Office*. Indianapolis: Bobbs-Merrill, 1945.

Motion Picture Association of America, Beverly Hills, Calif. MS file, "The Public Enemy."

Peary, Gerald. "More Than Meets the Eye: On William Wellman." *American Film*, March 1976.

Peary, Gerald. "The Rise of the American Gangster Film, 1913–1930." Ph.D. dissertation, University of Wisconsin, 1977.

Ryan, Mary P. "The Projection of a New Womanhood: The Movie Moderns in the 1920s," in Jean E. Friedman and William G. Shade, *Our American Sisters*. 2d ed. Boston: Allyn & Bacon, 1976.

Schickel, Richard. *The Men Who Made the Movies: Interviews*. New York: Atheneum, 1975.

Shulman, Irving. *Harlow: An Intimate Biography.* New York: Geis-Random House, 1964.

Silke, James R. *Here's Looking at You, Kid.* Boston: Little, Brown, 1976.

Steen, Mike. *Hollywood Speaks: An Oral History.* New York: Putnam, 1974.

Thomson, David. *A Biographical Dictionary of Film.* New York: Morrow, 1976.

Thrasher, Frederic Milton. *The Gang: A Study of 1,313 Gangs in Chicago.* Chicago: University of Chicago Press, 1927.

Walsh, Raoul. *Each Man in His Time: The Life Story of a Director.* New York: Farrar Straus Giroux, 1974.

Warshow, Robert. *The Immediate Experience.* New York: Atheneum, 1970.

Wellek, René. "Realism in Literature," in *Encyclopedia of the History of Ideas.* New York: Scribners, 1973.

Wellman, William A. *A Short Time for Insanity: An Autobiography.* New York: Hawthorn, 1974.

Wellman, William A. *Go, Get 'Em!* Boston: Page, 1918.

Wellman, Jr., William. "William Wellman: Director Rebel." *Action,* March–April 1970.

Illustrations

The frame enlargements have been selected to show the main themes in *The Public Enemy*. They follow the chronology of the film.

I. The Sense of Place

Some of the stock shots that introduce the movie (figures 1–4) suggest Chicago of the 1920s, particularly the shots of the elevated train station (not shown) and the stockyards. Nevertheless, the quickly paced scenes and sounds (the latter brought vividly to eye in figure 4) capture the mundane feeling of any American industrial city of the time. Backgrounds recurrently extend this feeling to working-class residential neighborhood, department store, warehouse and factory district, back alley (figures 5, 6, 7, 13, 18, 19). The glamourous is juxtaposed to the ordinary and the tawdry (figures 14 and 28). The execution is skillful and economical.

II. Authority

Explicitly by the policeman's hat, implicitly by camera angle, equations are drawn or implied: society and police, family and father (6, 7, 8, 9). The wordless impersonality and remote presence of authority, compounded by temptations and by the restraints and punishments, explain and provoke young Tom's defiance: "How do ya want 'em this time, up or down?" (10, 11, 12).

III. Heirs: The War of Brothers

The tensions between Mike and Tom (22), with the elder as heir to their father's authority and values and to his conflict with Tom, are vividly enacted. Ma Powers can only behold her sons' battles helplessly (32).

IV. Masculinism and Rebellion

Sight and sound collaborate to catalog Tom's war upon gentility: against manners (20, 21); booze (23); sex (24); the pool room and easy money vs. the school and hard work (15—"He's learnin' how to be poor"); against patriotism (and grammar!) (26—"Your hands ain't so clean!").

Many of the basic conflicts that drive the movie are summed up in an arresting composition, at once ominous and comic (25).

V. Buddies

Tom and Matt are friend and foil in life and death (6, 13, 15, 16, 17, 21, 33). Contrast these pairings with those of Tom and Mike (22, 32).

VI. Women and Their Places

They vary widely, in their half of the binary world (though in different degrees they share a common ineffectuality when they try to influence the men): from maternal and domestic (10, 32) to glamourous cafe society partners (28, the most populous shot in the film), "broad" (24, 27), goddess (30–31), true love (29—with Mamie's very mixed feelings as she agrees with Matt's "I guess Tom ain't the marryin' kind").

VII. Toughness and Fear

The toughness is there, in Tom, from as early as we see him (12). Fear comes as he watches Matt die (34).

VIII. Cycles: Violence, Retribution, Death

Society, in the family, struck first (10, 11, 12); Mike's patriotic hands "ain't so clean" (26); the law shot first (18, 19). Outlaw society also provokes its destiny: Putty Nose—his hand patting Matt's shoulder—advances toward his own doom; the gleam of those seduced by the gun is shown with an unsurpassed sinister allure (17).

The gangster glamour is given the lie; there is no pride in these deaths (19, 35, 36).

1. *Buildings and traffic (scene 1).*

2. *The busy city (scene 1).*

3. *The stockyards (scene 2).*

4. *A factory whistle (scene 3).*

5. A back-of-the-yards street (scene 5).

6. A floorwalker pursues Tom and Matt (scenes 9–10).

7. *Another authority figure in the department store (scenes 9–10).*

8. *Officer Powers (scene 25).*

9. *Tom understands his father's summoning stare (scene 26).*

10. *Getting the strap from the kitchen (scene 29).*

11. "How do ya want 'em this time, up or down?" (scene 32).

12. The beating (scene 32).

13. *The neighborhood hangout (scene 33).*

14. *Inside, Putty Nose entertains (scene 34).*

15. *Same buddies, same place, several years later (scene 40).*

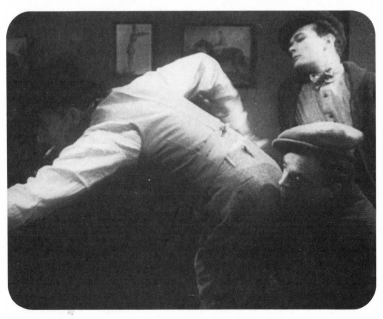

16. *Pool at the Red Oaks (scene 40).*

17. *Bliss in the back room (scene 41).*

18. *Gunfire in the alley (scene 51).*

19. *A death in the alley (after scene 54).*

20. *Paddy Ryan, proprietor (scene 66).*

21. *Spitting makes a point at Paddy's saloon (scene 66).*

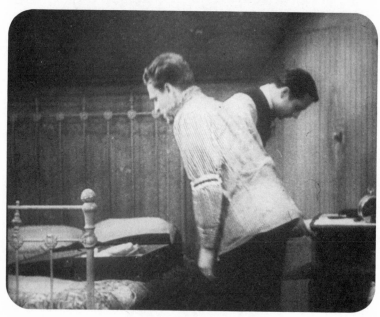

22. *Tom and Mike at home (scene 68).*

23. *Tom, Paddy, and Matt drink to prosperity (scene 84).*

24. *Tom and Kitty's first meeting (scene 108).*

25. *A special centerpiece to welcome Mike home (scene 126).*

26. *The family dinner ends (scene 131).*

27. *Squush: the film's most famous shot (scene 137).*

28. *Nails Nathan's party arrives (scene 145).*

29. *"I guess Tom ain't the marryin' kind." "No . . . I guess not "* (scene 149).

30. *Tom and Gwen at her apartment (scene 163).*

31. *"You're different, Tommy . . . very different" (scene 163).*

32. *The brothers' war rages (scene 169).*

33. *Machine gun fire strikes Matt (after scene 188).*

34. *Tom takes cover (scene 189).*

35. *Matt dies in agony (scene 191).*

36. *Tom comes home (scene 217).*

The Public Enemy

Screenplay
by
HARVEY THEW

Based on the novel by
KUBEC GLASMON
and
JOHN BRIGHT

The Public Enemy

TITLE: 1909

FADE IN ON

1.   A LONG SHOT OF THE CHICAGO LAKEFRONT
panning around to get the skyline of the tall buildings, towers, etc., the traffic at the mouth of the river, the smoke, and general effect of the busy city.

As we come in on the SHOT, we hear in the distance the roar of traffic and the city noises rising throughout the whole.

LAP DISSOLVE TO:

2.   STOCK SHOT OF THE UNION STOCKYARDS
Should be a LONG SHOT taken from a height overlooking the yards, or possibly a moving AERIAL SHOT picking up prominently the sign Union Stockyards.

The noises of traffic and industry continue through the SHOT and are suddenly pierced by the sound of a factory whistle.

LAP DISSOLVE TO:

3.   CLOSE-UP OF FACTORY WHISTLE BLOWING

LAP DISSOLVE TO:

4.   STOCKYARDS GATE
Crowds of workmen are beginning to pour out of the yards, carrying their coats over their arms, lunch boxes and dinner pails, some chattering together in groups, others moving more slowly and wearily, all of them cheered and relieved by the end of the long day's toil. They hurry away in all directions.

LAP DISSOLVE TO:

5.   A RESIDENTIAL STREET
A traveling shot on a street typical of the thoroughfares

back of the yards . . . ill-kept yards and squatted houses. Laborers hurrying along with their coats over their arms and lunch boxes in their hands.

Laborers' wives calling to one another from windows, children playing in the streets, squabbling over marbles, batting balls, etc. Other children and an occasional woman dashing down the street with empty beer pails hurrying for the evening beer.

LAP DISSOLVE TO:

6.   BUSINESS STREET

TRUCK THE CAMERA along the middle of the street, shooting at the store fronts to show that almost every other building is an old-time saloon. (The period of this time is about 1909.)

The saloon signs show that the proprietors are all sharply contrasted nationalities. The first one reads Adolph Krausmeyer; the second, Boris Stepovitch. On each of them, beer signs are prominent.

The crowds of workmen on their way home hurry eagerly into their favorite saloons. We hear the street noises off-scene and in the distance the music of a small Salvation Army band.

7.   CLOSE-UP OF A ROW OF BEER SPIGOTS BEHIND A BAR

with just the hands of a bartender rapidly filling tin pails, which he slides along in a row, scraping the suds off of each one and sliding it on.

Off-scene we hear the babble of voices of men gathering at the bar, calling, "Two beers here, Joe," "Make mine a dark," "Rush 'em along, Joe," etc., ad lib.

8.   BUSINESS STREET

We continue the TRUCKING SHOT, presumably now in another block. The same business of pedestrians, laborers, hurrying into the saloons; women and children with beer pails. The saloon signs read Morris Bernstein's Palace, O'Leary's Famous Bar, Stockyards Saloon.

We hear the chatter of voices, the music of the band, and as we pass along, pick up a small Salvation Army group singing at the curb. The pedestrians, intent on their evening beer, pay little attention to the workers.

We reach the corner occupied by a saloon busier than the rest. Sign says Patrick J. Ryan. Customers hurrying in and out of the entrance at the corner. CAMERA TRUCKS around the corner to the side and stops at the door marked Family Entrance. Immediately two boys, Tom and Matt—Matt about eleven, Tom, ten—come out of the family entrance, Matt carefully carrying a pail of beer, both of them nibbling on pretzels. Tom looks around quickly to see if anyone is watching, turns to Matt.

TOM:
Gimme a swig.

Matt jerks a hasty look up and down the street, hands the pail to Tom, who quickly takes a gulp of beer. As he returns the pail, the two girls we saw leaving with a beer pail from the residential street enter with the pail. Matt grins but Tom shies away as though he didn't want to talk to them.

FIRST GIRL:
Hello, Tommy.

TOMMY (ill at ease, starting to walk away):
'Lo.

MATT (more friendly, looks into the girl's pail):
Can greased?

He quickly runs his finger around inside the pail and nods.

SECOND GIRL (looking at Tom, who is standing a few feet off, hovering about uneasy):
What's the matter with Tom, Matt?

MATT (looking at Tom):
He don't go for girls . . . that's all.

FIRST GIRL:
> Nor for school either. He ain't been there for a week.

TOM (scowling):
> C'mon, Matt. We got business.

Matt playfully tweaks the hair of one of the girls, turns, and joins Tom. Tom gives him a scornful look as they walk off. The girls give them a look over their shoulder, then enter the family entrance.[1]

FADE OUT

FADE IN

9.   INT. DEPARTMENT STORE   MED. SHOT ON A DESCENDING ESCALATOR

Number of customers scattered along the runway, most of them with packages in their hands, descending. Tom and Matt run in at the foot of the escalator, pursued by big bruiserlike floorwalker who is scowling at them savagely. They jump onto the escalator and, running against the descending motion, duck between the customers, making their way toward the top.

The floorwalker is slowed up by the traffic on the escalator but continues to pursue after the boys. He is furiously angry.

10.   DEPARTMENT STORE   CLOSE SHOT AT TOP OF ESCALATOR

The boys, darting between the customers, who give exclamations of annoyance, reach the top of the escalator. They exchange grins of triumph as they start away.

We PAN over with them. They find themselves facing another floorwalker, more threatening than the first. They stop in their tracks, sunk for a moment, then Tom makes a leap for the escalator and catches the descending rail. Matt eagerly gets the idea, and as the floorwalker makes a grab for him, he follows Tom.

11.   DEPARTMENT STORE   MED. SHOT ON THE ESCALATOR

PAN with the boys as they slide rapidly down the rail,

their speed increasing by its own descending motion. Halfway down, they meet the first floorwalker. He is prevented from grabbing them by a couple of customers coming between him and the rail. The boys slide past him at high speed. He turns back after them.

12.   DEPARTMENT STORE   AT THE FOOT OF THE ESCALATOR
As the boys slide down off the end of the rail, an elderly man with both arms full of packages is stepping off and is keeping his balance with difficulty on account of the number of packages he holds before him. As Tom passes, he grabs the man's hat, takes it off, and lays it on top of the pile of packages.

The man stares furiously at them; both hands are full, and he can't replace his hat. The boys grin and start away, putting on an elaborately careless air like ordinary shoppers.

TRUCK CAMERA after them down the aisle. They pass a counter loaded with odds and ends of kitchen utensils, and as they pass, Tom reaches out without looking, grabs the first thing he sees without pausing.

INSERT   CLOSE-UP OF TOM'S HAND
seizing a set of cheap pepper and salt shakers from the counter and stuffing them into his pocket.

BACK TO SCENE:
The boys continue on down the aisle, stuffing the salt and pepper shakers into their pockets. TRUCK with them until they come to the end of the aisle where another aisle crosses it, leaving a dead wall ahead. They stop, look up toward one of the cross aisles.

13.   DEPARTMENT STORE
A FLASH of the end of the aisle, with a lighted sign which says Sporting Goods.

14.   DEPARTMENT STORE   CLOSE SHOT ON TOM AND MATT
They turn to look from the sporting goods section and

glance in another direction. FLASH at other end of aisle a lighted sign reads Women's Apparel.

15. CLOSE SHOT ON TOM AND MATT
Matt is about to start toward sporting goods department. Tom gives him a quick wink toward the other direction and they walk carelessly off toward the women's department.

A moment later the first floorwalker appears. He looks up and down the aisle. The sporting goods sign tells him that that is, of course, the direction the boys took and he hurries off toward it. Bring groups of shoppers through from both directions to make it plausible that the floorwalker can't see the boys.

16. DEPARTMENT STORE   WOMEN'S DEPARTMENT
Typical display of women's intimate garments. Tables of lingerie, bust forms, etc., displaying undergarments, brassieres, and the like. Number of shoppers examining merchandise.

Tom and Matt saunter in carelessly, considering themselves well hidden in such a place. Matt nudges Tom and indicates a bust on one of the counters. They examine it with interest, making elaborate bows to it. Both have a rather embarrassed interest in the suggestion of the female form. Matt edges up close to the bust, reaches out, and is about to feel the shoulders and breast when the salesgirl comes up.

SALESGIRL (smiling; slightly ironic):
Can I show you something, gentlemen?

TOM:
Naw . . . we seen something already.

He pulls Matt away. Salesgirl smiles, realizing the boys have gotten into the wrong department. As soon as her back is turned, Tom snatches the nearest article from the counter. It proves to be a brassiere. He quickly stuffs it into his hip pocket, leaving one end of it dangling. The boys resume their careless manner and stroll out.

FADE OUT

FADE IN

17. BACK ALLEY   CLOSE SHOT OF TOM AND MATT
hiding behind the dilapidated building, looking over their loot. Matt is puffing at a brand new pipe while Tom is pulling the salt and pepper shakers out of his pocket. The pipe is empty but both of the boys are admiring it.

MATT:
    Try it.

He hands pipe to Tom, who sets down the shakers.

TOM (pulling on pipe):
    Draws swell.

MATT (examining shakers):
    What are we goin' to do with these?

TOM (laconically):
    Hide 'em.

MATT:
    They ain't much good.

TOM:
    I know . . . wanna see somethin'? (He pulls out the skates.)

MATT (seizing one of them):
    Oh, boy! (Tries one on his shoe.)

TOM:
    Your feet are too big.

Tom tries on the other one, which is too small for him also.

MATT:
    Your clodhoppers ain't any smaller.

TOM:
> I'll get a bigger pair next time.

MATT:
> We ain't goin' there no more.

TOM:
> I'll say we ain't. (Matt notices the brassiere and pulls it out, laughing.) I got that for you.

MATT (derisively):
> Did'ja? I bet you don't even know what it's for.

TOM (with an obscene leer):
> No?

He adjusts it to Matt, whose hands are full. Matt pushes him away.

TOM (holding up the brassiere and mimicking the sales-girl):
> Can I show you something, gentlemen? (Both boys laugh uproariously.)[2]

FADE OUT

FADE IN

18.   EXT. POWERS HOME   CLOSE SHOT OF MOLLY

A girl of ten, bareheaded with pigtail braids hanging down her back. She has the roller skates on and is struggling to master them. The sidewalk is in a rickety condition. There are patches of wooden sidewalk between patches of stone or brick.

The street is in dilapidated condition with mud holes at the curb and litter of all kinds strewn around.

Molly has never been on skates before and is having all she can do to stand up. We PAN over and show Tom sitting at the edge of the sidewalk in front of the Powers house.

The house is a rather ramshackle wooden affair like most of the houses in the district with a high porch and wooden sidewalk in front.

Tom has tied a strong cord to a nail in the steps an

inch or so above the level of the sidewalk and has laid the cord in the crack between two boards and has hold of the other end as by drawing it tight he can raise it and trip Molly as she comes past. Matt is standing near, watching him with an air of protest.

19.   EXT. POWERS HOME   CLOSE SHOT ON TOM AND MATT

Tom with a grin shows Matt how the cord works. He darts a look at Molly, who is a few yards down the sidewalk, pulls the string tight, looks up at Matt for approval. His manner shows that he takes delight in playing mean tricks. In fact, we may infer that is the reason he gave Molly the skates.

MATT (in low voice):
Aw, Tom . . . that ain't fair.

TOM (scornfully):
What do you care? It's only a girl.

MATT:
She's my sister.

TOM:
What difference does that make?

Matt looks away toward Molly, is about to protest further, when Tom gives him a threatening look which tells him to keep his mouth shut. We see that Matt is accustomed to follow Tom's lead, and he keeps still.

Molly skates into the scene holding on to the fence or whatever there is that she can use to keep her balance. Tom waits tensely, ready to pull the string.

MOLLY:
Hold me up, Matt.

Matt instinctively starts, takes a step toward her.

TOM:
She's doin' all right. That's the way to learn.

Matt hesitates; Tom gives him a threatening look. Matt

decides not to go to Molly's aid. As Molly passes the steps there is nothing for her to hold on to and she has to go on her own. She wavers and staggers but gets ahead and is all ready to reach for the rail on the other side of the step when Tom suddenly pulls the string taut and trips her. She falls in a heap. Tom laughs. Matt joins him. Molly sits up angrily.

MOLLY:
> That's just like you, Tom Powers! You're the meanest boy in town.

MATT (as Tom laughs):
> No, he ain't. He give you the skates, didn't he?

MOLLY:
> I believe he did it just so he could play that trick on me.

Tom merely laughs as Molly struggles to get to her feet, holding on to the fence, having a lot of trouble about it.

MOLLY:
> I'm gonna tell your brother Mike.

TOM (scornfully):
> Go on and tell him. Here he comes now.

He nods his head toward the corner of the house.

20.   OUTSIDE POWERS HOUSE   CLOSE SHOT ON MIKE
coming around the corner from the back yard. Mike is about fourteen, a different type from Tom, more of a serious and studious sort. He stops a moment, sees the little group on the sidewalk, and comes over.

21.   OUTSIDE POWERS HOUSE   MED. SHOT ON TOM, MATT,
AND MOLLY
Molly has gotten to her feet and is holding onto the fence. Tom is still sitting on the edge of the sidewalk as Mike walks in.

MOLLY (to Mike):
  You'll help me, won't you, Mike?

MIKE:
  Where'd you get the skates, Molly?

MOLLY:
  Tom gave 'em to me.

Tom turns his face away, sullen. He knows from experience that Mike is going to interfere and he resents it.

MIKE (surprised):
  Tom did? (Turns to look at Tom.) Where'd *you* get 'em, Tom?

Tom keeps his face turned away sullenly and ignores the question.

MOLLY:
  He got 'em from a kid who owed him some money.

22.   OUTSIDE POWERS HOUSE   CLOSE-UP OF MIKE
He turns to again look at Tom, suspicion growing on him. Turns and walks over toward Tom.

23.   OUTSIDE POWERS HOUSE   CLOSE SHOT ON TOM AND MIKE
Molly and Matt in background.

MIKE (looking at Tom accusingly):
  Tom . . . I bet you stole 'em!

Tom returns his gaze boldly and doesn't reply. Mike is now convinced he is right. He turns to Molly.

MIKE:
  Give 'em back, Molly.

TOM (getting to his feet):
  Why don't you mind your own business? No one asked you to put your two cents in!

He walks away toward the house.

24.   OUTSIDE POWERS HOUSE   MED. SHOT ON THE GROUP

Tom walks over and leans against the fence in elaborate indifference. Mike is looking steadily at Molly, doing forced demands. Molly hesitates. She doesn't want to give up the skates but sees she'll have to. She sits down on the steps and starts unstrapping them.

MOLLY (in low voice):
> Here, Tom. I don't want 'em if you stole them.

She has one skate off and holds it up to Tom.

TOM:
> So you're gettin' like sissy Mike too!

MOLLY (lays skate on the steps):
> Take 'em Tom.

TOM (resentfully):
> Say, you're not so darn good. Your old man swipes pigeons.

MOLLY (stops in the act of unbuttoning other skate; looks up indignantly):
> Tom Powers, he does not! You're a big liar!

TOM:
> Well . . . he's in jail, ain't he? And they don't send people there for nothin'!

MOLLY (with growing indignation):
> Everybody who belongs there ain't there. That's where you'll be some day, Tom Powers!

TOM (about to turn away):
> Well . . . I ain't there yet. And if I do go, it won't be for stealing pigeons!

He turns away with a lofty air when something in the door of the house catches his eye.

25.   OUTSIDE POWERS HOME   CLOSE SHOT AT THE DOORWAY

Powers, Sr., is standing in the doorway. He is a uniformed policeman, but now he is in shirtsleeves, wearing the pants and the policeman's cap on the back of his head. He stares steadily at Tom and we see that he has overheard the whole conversation.

26.   OUTSIDE POWERS HOME   CLOSE-UP OF TOM
He catches his father's eye. He knows what this means. It is an old situation for him. No words need be spoken. Instead of going down the street, he starts toward the steps with the air of one who knows what is coming and has to go through it as a matter of form.

27.   OUTSIDE POWERS HOME   CLOSE SHOT AT THE DOORWAY
Tom marches up the steps doggedly without looking at his father.[3] Powers, Sr., steps aside. Tom marches into the house. Powers turns in after him. The whole thing is done in matter-of-fact way as though it were a frequent occurrence.

28.   POWERS LIVING ROOM
Fairly large-sized room furnished in the style of a workman's home of that district and period. Tom marches through from the front door, his father following him, in the same mechanical, matter-of-fact way that they entered the house.

29.   POWERS KITCHEN   CLOSE-UP
of a razor strap hanging on a nail beside the sink. Powers's hand reaches in and takes down the strap.

30.   POWERS KITCHEN   CLOSE-UP OF TOM
staring stolidly at his father's hand as he gets the strap. A sullen smoldering look is in his eyes, but he has no intention of making any protest or of flinching.

31.   POWERS KITCHEN   MED. SHOT
Powers in the most matter-of-fact way possible motions to Tom to turn around. Tom turns and bends over a

chair. Powers raises the strap and brings it down with resounding quack on his rear end. He continues giving him a cruel beating.

32. POWERS KITCHEN CLOSE-UP OF TOM
just his face. His teeth are clenched hard. The same sullen smoldering look is in his eyes. He flinches involuntarily at each blow which we hear, but he is hard boiled and has no intention of letting out a yell or making any protest.[4]

FADE OUT

FADE IN

33. EXT. RED OAKS CLUB MED. SHOT
on the front of a ramshackle one-story detached building on a business street. It looks like an old abandoned store building. The windows are thick with grime, and there are heavy curtains behind them so that we don't see inside. A crude sign painted on a piece of wood across the door says Red Oaks Club.

Tom and Matt enter. Their manner is very furtive and sly. They both wear sweaters. Tom has something stuck under his sweater that he is trying to conceal.

As we come in on the scene we hear a piano inside the building banging out the air of "Frankie and Johnnie" and the coarse voice of Putty Nose singing the words. As Tom and Matt start into the building,

LAP DISSOLVE TO:

34. INT. RED OAKS CLUB
A large bare room, ill kept, plaster peeling from the walls and ceiling. The only furniture is a battered upright piano against one wall, two or three rickety tables, and about a half dozen rickety kitchen chairs.

Three or four boys about Tom's age are gathered around the table playing cards. A half dozen more are gathered around Putty Nose, who is at the piano banging on the keys and singing "Frankie and Johnnie" with

72

many sly winks and grimaces to bring out the suggestive part. The boys are hugely delighted.[5]

Tom and Matt enter from the street. They are anxious not to attract attention. They slip between the two groups of boys toward the back room, which is separated from the main room by a thin partition with one door. They steal into the back room, stand just inside the door, turn around, and try to catch Putty Nose's eye.

35. INT. RED OAKS CLUB   CLOSE SHOT
on Tom and Matt standing just inside the door in the back room waiting for a chance to signal Putty Nose. We hear Putty Nose off-scene singing "Frankie and Johnnie." Just before he gets to the filthiest part of the words, Tom catches his eye and gives him a signal that they want to see him privately. The music stops. There are cries from the boys off-scene, "Go on, Putty Nose," "Don't stop," "That's swell, Putty Nose," etc.

PUTTY NOSE (off-scene):
    Be back in a minute, boys.

He enters the SHOT. Tom and Matt back into the inner room and Putty Nose follows them in.

36. BACK ROOM OF CLUB
This is a small room which has been partitioned off from the main room and is used as Putty Nose's sleeping quarters. There is a cot underneath the window which has not been made up, an old valise open with Putty Nose's things scattered onto the edge of it over the floor, washstand with pitcher and bowl.

Tom and Matt standing just inside the door. Putty Nose walks in.

PUTTY NOSE:
    What's up, boys?

Tom with an air of great secrecy carefully closes the door.

MATT:

We got something.

Tom, making sure the door is closed, fumbles under his sweater and pulls out a showcard on which there are fastened six watches, evidently something stolen from the top of a store showcase. Putty Nose gives it an appraising glance.

PUTTY NOSE:

Where'd you get 'em?

TOM:

Wentworth Avenue.

MATT:

How much are they worth?

PUTTY NOSE (he examines the watches contemptuously for business reasons):

Not much. Just cheap watches.

TOM (indignantly):

Cheap watches? A buck apiece.

MATT:

And there's six of 'em.

PUTTY NOSE:

I don't know what I can do with 'em. They ain't new . . . and they're hot.

TOM:

Aw, quit stalling, Putty Nose. You know how to sell 'em.

PUTTY NOSE (laughing):

You're too smart. Well . . . I'll see what I can do.

TOM:

How much do we get?

PUTTY NOSE (considers as the boys watch him intently; puts his hands in his pocket and brings up some silver):
> What do you say to half buck apiece?

TOM (scornfully):
> Half a buck?

PUTTY NOSE:
> I'm not cheatin' you, Tom. That's a good price. I have to take all the risk . . . and maybe I can't sell 'em at all.

TOM (impatiently):
> Give us the half buck.

PUTTY NOSE (as he gives each boy a quarter):
> You know old Putty Nose always plays on the square with you.

TOM (indignantly):
> Hey! This is only two bits.

PUTTY NOSE:
> Well, you both owe me a month's dues, don't you?

MATT:
> That's right, Tom.

PUTTY NOSE:
> So we're callin' that square . . . That's all right, ain't it?

MATT:
> Sure.

PUTTY NOSE (as he turns to hide the watches underneath the bedclothes):
> You done a good stroke of business. And if you find anything more . . .

He gives them a meaning look. Tom and Matt nod, turn toward the door.

                                              LAP DISSOLVE

37.   EXT. RED OAKS CLUB   MED. SHOT

Tom and Matt come out. They stand in front of the building a moment without speaking, each holding his quarter, trying to decide what to do with it. Inside the piano suddenly strikes up again with "Frankie and Johnnie," and Putty Nose starts singing another verse.

FADE OUT

FADE IN

38.   TITLE: 1915

OUTSIDE RED OAKS CLUB

The same shot and the same angle as before, but the time is now seven years later and the building shows the changes of its time. It has been spruced up and a much better sign reads Red Oaks Social Club. Painted on the windows are the words Cigars and Cigarettes, Pool.

Tom and Matt, now seventeen and eighteen years old, are standing almost in the same spot they occupied in the previous scene. They have just arrived. We use their positions to partially identify them as Tom and Matt grown seven years older. They wear sweaters and caps on the sides of their heads and carry themselves with the slouching walk of the young loafer. They start into the building.

LAP DISSOLVE TO:

39.   INT. CIGAR STORE

This is the front of the old clubroom partitioned off to make a small room in which there is a cigar case, a few shelves, and a small stock of cigars and cigarettes. The place is in somewhat better condition than the original Red Oaks Club, but is the low-class cigar counter.

Hack Miller, a young man of the hoodlum type and several years older than Tom and Matt, is behind the counter as Matt and Tom enter. Tom questions Hack silently with raised eyebrows, and Hack makes a motion with his head toward the back room. Tom and Matt exit to the back room.

40.   INT. CLUBROOM

The old room is slightly smaller on account of the front partition. There is a pool table and couple of card tables. Putty Nose with Dutch Sieberling, Bugs Healey, and Limpy Larry are gathered in a little group talking in whispers. Limpy, Bugs, and Dutch are hoodlum types, some few years older than Tom and Matt. Limpy walks with a pronounced limp.

DUTCH (growls):
    What do we want with a couple of young squirts like them?

PUTTY NOSE:
    They ain't gonna be so bad . . . and they won't expect much of a cut . . .

Tom and Matt enter with a little swagger and the group quickly separates apart. Putty puts on a welcome smile.

PUTTY NOSE:
    Hey there, Tom.

TOM:
    'Lo, Putty.

PUTTY NOSE (looking back at the door):
    Are you alone?

TOM:
    I'm always alone when I'm with Matt.

MATT (good-naturedly to Tom):
    You lookin' for a sock in the button?

PUTTY NOSE (ironically):
    I was afraid he might bring Mike.

TOM (in deep scorn):
    That sucker! He's too busy . . . goin' to school.[6]

PUTTY NOSE:
    Ain't he workin' on the streetcars anymore?

TOM:

Sure. He's the ding-dong in the day time. School at night.

MATT:

What did you want, Putty?

PUTTY NOSE:

Something sweet. (He comes over and puts his arms around the shoulders of Tom and Matt and pulls their heads toward his.) 'Member I always said when I got something good I'd cut you in?

TOM (distrustingly):

Yeah?

PUTTY NOSE:

Well . . .

He looks around at the other hoodlums who are waiting silently, then motions with his thumb toward the back room as though this was too private to be discussed here. He starts for the back room and the others follow.

LAP DISSOLVE TO:

41. BACK ROOM OF CLUB

The room is practically the same as we last saw it. Putty Nose, Tom, Matt, Dutch, Limpy, and Bugs are gathered in a close group on the bed and in chairs, just finishing a discussion which has been going on in low tones with their heads together. Putty Nose has evidently been trying to sell his argument to Tom and Matt. The others appear to know all about it.

PUTTY NOSE:

Dutch here knows the whole layout. We've been casing the joint for a whole week.

TOM:

But . . . suppose the cops . . .

PUTTY NOSE (ribbing):

You ain't afraid of cops. Besides, old Putty Nose'll

take care of ya, won't he? (With a nod toward Limpy.) Limpy will be lookout. The place is dead at night anyhow. (Pause.) Well . . . are ya on?

MATT (interested but hesitant):
We ain't ever done nothin' so big . . .

PUTTY NOSE:
Big is right. I'm givin' ya a break like I promised. Furs . . . furs is worth plenty nowadays. How about you, Tom?

TOM (hesitates):
It's sort of new stuff for me.

PUTTY NOSE:
Ya gotta grow up sometime. (With a sudden idea.) Here! (Gets up quickly and goes to drawer of rickety dresser, brings out two new pistols.) Christmas present from Santa Claus.

Hands one to Tom and one to Matt. They take them with the amazed wonder of children getting an unexpected present. Putty Nose stands beaming on them. The other hoodlums watch them a little tolerantly.

42. CLOSE SHOT ON TOM AND MATT
sitting close together, each examining his pistol with wonder and delight. They try the feel of it, turn it over, examine it on all sides, then they look up and meet each other's gaze. Their eyes shining, their expressions tell us that they are completely won over to Putty's proposition.

FADE OUT

FADE IN
43. EXT. FUR WAREHOUSE   NIGHT
On an establishing SHOT. Corner of a three- or four-story dingy brick building with sign Northwestern Fur Trading Company dimly seen in poorly lighted street.

LAP DISSOLVE TO:

44.   INT. WAREHOUSE
We see only what is shown in the circle of a flashlight moving rapidly along the wall, showing piles of fur piled on top of one another. Other piles on the floor.

45.   ALLEY   MED. SHOT AT THE MOUTH OF A DARK ALLEY
Just inside the shadows we see the suggestion of a truck waiting, and nearby is Limpy on watch.

46.   INT. FUR WAREHOUSE   MED. SHOT
We see only the circle of lights from three or four flash-lights moving around from different sides of the room. One of the men with flashlight is rapidly selecting bales of furs and hauling them out onto the floor. Tom, hold-ing his flashlight with one hand and his pistol with the other, comes into foreground so that we see him only in silhouette against the light from other flashlights in background.

Tom is alert and tense, excited by the unusual experi-ence. One of the other flashlights sweeping about the room picks him up suddenly with a flood of light and he gives a nervous jump.[7] The light passes on leaving him in darkness.

47.   INT. WAREHOUSE   CLOSE SHOT ON TOM
We shoot from behind and see him silhouetted against the light from his own flashlight, which he is throwing on the wall in front of him.

48.   INT. WAREHOUSE   CLOSE-UP
of the circle of light from Tom's flashlight. It suddenly picks up the grinning face of a stuffed bear standing upright on a pedestal.

49.   INT. WAREHOUSE   CLOSE-UP OF TOM
his face seen dimly in reflected light, sudden look of alarm and terror. Instinctively he fires three or four shots in rapid succession at the bear.

50. INT. WAREHOUSE FULL SHOT
Confusion of muttered exclamations and curses. The lights flash rapidly all over the room, then go out. We hear the scramble of feet toward the door, confusion of muttered exclamations.

51. ALLEY MED. SHOT
Limpy looking wildly about. He starts away in a limping run. As he disappears in the darkness we hear policeman's voice off-scene:

POLICEMAN (off-scene):
    Stop there! Stop! I'll shoot!

The policeman runs into the scene, his eyes intent on the direction Limpy has taken.

POLICEMAN:
    Stop, I said!

He pulls his gun and fires after Limpy.

52. STREET CLOSE SHOT
at a corner lighted by a streetlamp. Limpy stumbles into the light of the lamp, staggers for a moment, then falls.

53. EXT. WAREHOUSE CLOSE SHOT ON THE POLICEMAN
running along the building, looking for an entrance. He turns back, sees someone at the other corner of the building.

POLICEMAN (shouting):
    Hey there! Where you going!? Stop!

He dashes off in pursuit.

54. ALLEY
A SHOT at the mouth of the alley. There is a dim light in the foreground but the alley itself is in pitch darkness. Tom and Matt come running around the corner of the building, scared stiff. They see the policeman. Tom ducks into the alley, Matt follows.

The policeman dashes in from the opposite side with his pistol ready. He chases into the alley after the boys and disappears in the darkness. We hear a shot; it is quickly followed by two others in quick succession, then a scream.

55.   STREET   CLOSE SHOT AT THE OUTER END OF THE ALLEY
There is a dim light in the foreground, but the alley itself is pitch black. We hold the SHOT empty for a second, then Tom and Matt run out, stop in the foreground breathless, exchange significant, terrified glances. They make a quick survey of the street and throw their guns away. Tom motions for Matt to follow and they slink off down the street rapidly, keeping close to the wall.

FADE OUT

FADE IN

56.   REAR OF RED OAKS CLUB   ALLEY   DAWN
It is very dirty and disfigured with broken-down fences, ash cans, and piles of refuse. Tom and Matt enter, clothes disarrayed, faces showing fear mingled with excitement. They enter yard and knock on door. There is a ray of light from a vertical crack. They knock three times—no answer. Tom walks over and impatiently knocks on window.

MATT (calling softly):
    Putty . . . Putty Nose. (They wait a moment.)

TOM:
    Where is that big loogan?

A voice from inside answers.

VOICE (off-scene):
    Who is it?

TOM:
    Us.

The door opens and instead of Putty we see Hack Miller.

MATT:
>   Where's Putty? We knocked off . . . (Tom nudges
>   him sharply.)

HACK (grinning):
>   I know all about it. Putty lammed. You better lay
>   low for a while. The heat's goin' to be on.[8] (Lifts
>   eyebrows significantly.)

Instead of an answer the door slowly closes. Tom and
Matt face each other. Tom puts a cigarette in his mouth.

TOM (with tense fury):
>   That dirty no good yellow-bellied stool! I'll give it
>   to that Putty Nose right in the head, the first time
>   I see him. (He lights match and raises it to his face.)

56A.   CLOSE-UP OF TOM
his hands cupping the lighted match illuminating his
face. His hand is shaking, showing great agitation.

FADE OUT

FADE IN

57.   INT. DALTON HOME   DAY
A poverty-stricken home, little better than a slum. A
pine box coffin propped up at one side so we won't see
into it. Several women seated in a semicircle of chairs in
front of it. Mrs. Dalton is sobbing. Mrs. Powers sits on
one side of her and Mrs. Doyle on the other. Mrs.
Dalton is sobbing and moaning. The other two women
pat her hand and try to comfort her. Mrs. Dalton keeps
repeating, "Poor Larry, he was a good boy." The others
sit stiff and stark, staring at the coffin.

58.   DALTON KITCHEN
Pat Burke, plainclothesman, and four or five of the men
are standing around the sink where a keg of beer is
propped up with a spigot. They are helping themselves
repeatedly. There is a great contrast between their manner and that of the women in the next room.

A MAN (as he draws a glass of beer):
> Well, it's here today and gone tomorrow.

BURKE:
> Well, Larry asked for it. I warned him.

ANOTHER MAN (drawing a glass of beer):
> He was a no good guy.

MRS. DALTON (voice off-scene moaning):
> Poor Larry, he was a good boy.

59. STREET
Near the Dalton house. TRAVELING SHOT on Tom and
Matt. They are uncomfortably dressed in ill-fitting
"Sunday clothes," walking along slowly and unwill-
ingly and talking in low voices.

MATT:
> Gee, I hate to go in there.

TOM:
> We got to. Just for the looks of it.

MATT (pause):
> I wonder which one of us give it to that cop.

TOM:
> What's the diff? You or me . . . or both of us? He
> had it coming.[9]

LAP DISSOLVE TO:

60. INT. DALTON HOME
The women are seated as before around the pine coffin.
Tom and Matt wander through, ill at ease, their hats in
their hands.

MRS. DALTON (moaning):
> Poor Larry. He was a good boy.

MRS. DOYLE (soothingly):
> He just got into bad company, that's all.

MRS. POWERS (sees Tom and Matt):
Come here, Tommy.

Tom goes over uneasily, Matt following a few steps behind.

MRS. POWERS (taking Tom's hand):
I'm glad you came, Tommy boy. Mrs. Dalton will be glad to see some of Larry's nicer friends.

She takes Tom's hand and puts it into the hand of Mrs. Dalton, who doesn't look up.

FADE OUT

TITLE: 1917
FADE IN

61. CLOSE-UP OF PRINTING PRESSES
running at full speed.

LAP DISSOLVE TO:

FRONT PAGE OF NEWSPAPER
with screaming headlines announcing that U.S. Declares War with picture of President Wilson, etc.

LAP DISSOLVE TO:

62. EXT. PADDY'S SALOON
The same SHOT we use in our opening scenes. There are several knots of men on the sidewalks with newspapers, eagerly discussing the war. As they flutter the newspaper we should catch the word *war* in large type on the front page in the foreground. We hear the babble of voices. Someone raises an argument, but we do not distinguish the words.

An Express Company truck drives up to the curb in foreground, cutting off the scene on the sidewalk. Tom is behind the wheel as driver, Matt beside him as helper. They wear the usual caps and badges, showing they are employed by the Express Company.

63. CLOSE SHOT ON MATT AND TOM
in the cab of the Express truck. Tom sets his brake as

Matt starts to get out. Matt sees someone on the sidewalk he wants to avoid, ducks back into the cab just as Tom is starting to climb out.

MATT (in low voice):
Wait a minute, Tom. Here comes Mike.

Tom scowls and peeks out of the cab. They both press back into the cab so as not to be seen.

64.   SIDEWALK   CLOSE SHOT OF MIKE AND MOLLY
Mike is in a streetcar conductor's uniform and carries a lunch box. Molly has hold of his arm. We play Mike from here on as about twenty-three and Molly nineteen. She is a good type of pretty, middle-class Irish girl who has a job and keeps herself looking attractive and respectable. They are both silent and thoughtful as though they have something of great importance on their minds. As they mingle with the other pedestrians on the sidewalk, they come into the foreground and stop. Mike, greatly troubled, hesitates a moment.

MIKE:
I wish you'd come home with me, Molly. I . . . I don't just know how to tell Ma.

MOLLY:
All right, Mike.

She takes his arm again and they go on.

65.   CLOSE SHOT ON TOM AND MATT IN THEIR CAB
keeping out of sight as they watch Mike and Molly.

TOM (sneering):
That sister of yours ain't getting any bargain in Mike.

MATT:
How come he ain't workin'?

TOM (with sneer):
> Probably been fired for snatching too many nickels.

MATT:
> They look like something happened.

TOM (watching Mike and Molly out of sight):
> C'mon. We gotta see Paddy.

He and Matt climb out of the cab, go toward Paddy's saloon.

LAP DISSOLVE TO:

66.   PADDY'S OFFICE   REAR OF SALOON

This is a little room off the back room with an old-fashioned rolltop desk and a couple of chairs. It is where Paddy makes up his few accounts. Paddy is now seated at his desk, turned to face Tom and Matt, who are seated awkwardly beside the desk. Paddy has been listening to them with a patient, fatherly air.

Paddy is a quiet man who suggests great force, the type of old-time political saloonkeeper, wise in the ways of the world.

PADDY:
> You don't need to stall with . . . Paddy Ryan, boys. I've been watching you . . . since you bought your first drink from me . . . and I know what you've been doing.

TOM:
> Well . . . it's like this, Paddy. We delivered some cigars today, must be worth twenty-five hundred.

Tom stops. Paddy merely nods as though to say, "Go on," watching the boys keenly. Tom hesitates, turns to Matt.

MATT:
> Took 'em to a place on Sixty-third . . . and was told to put 'em in the back.

TOM:

>We could lift 'em easily tonight.

Paddy nods as the boys wait for a reply, but Paddy means to let the boys do the talking.

MATT:

>Only . . . we don't know what to do with 'em.

Paddy lights a cigar and blows out a big cloud of smoke.

TOM (irritated at Paddy's silence):
>You sell cigars, don't you?

PADDY:

>Not that kind. Can't afford it. I have my own system, boys. But being a fence isn't part of it.

MATT (uneasy):
>Well . . . we thought maybe you knew somebody . . .

PADDY (nods, whispers in ear):
>Maybe I do.

TOM:

>Yeah.

PADDY:

>You might take 'em there. I'll call up and say you're coming.

MATT (sticks out his hand eagerly):
>Thanks, Paddy.

Matt and Tom get up, start away.

PADDY (stops them with a gesture):
>If you get into a jam, give me a ring. You'll find Paddy Ryan's your friend.

MATT (warmly):
>Thanks, Paddy.

TOM (suspiciously):
> Why do you want to front for us? We ain't done nothin' for you.

PADDY (putting his arm on Tom's shoulder):
> Maybe not. But I may need a friend myself sometime. I'm older than you, and I've learned that nobody can do much without somebody else. Remember this, boys . . . you gotta have friends. I've been watchin' you and hearin' about you . . . and I've been worried. I was worried when you got mixed up with that two-timer Putty Nose. Such guys are dangerous. I'm glad you come to me. So far as Paddy Ryan is concerned there's only two kinds of people . . . right and wrong. I think you're right and you'll find that I am . . . unless you cross me. That's all.

TOM (admiringly):
> Gee, Paddy . . . that's swell.

Paddy extends his hand and Tom grasps it, his face lighting up as though he had recognized a new and wonderful lesson.

FADE OUT

FADE IN

67. INT. POWERS LIVING ROOM   DAY
Mrs. Powers is sitting in a chair weeping softly, and Molly is standing beside her stroking her hair, trying to cheer her up. Tom enters from the street. At first he doesn't know what is going on.

TOM:
> 'Lo, Ma . . .

He stops suddenly, notices something is wrong.

MRS. POWERS (jumping up at sound of his voice):
> Oh Tommy . . . Tommy boy.

She runs over and throws her arms about him. Tom looks very uncomfortable. Looks away toward Molly for an explanation.

MRS. POWERS:
>You won't leave me, Tommy, will you? You're all I got left, Tommy boy.

TOM (uncomfortably):
>What's wrong, Ma? (To Molly.) What's up?

MOLLY (quietly):
>Mike's enlisted.

TOM (speechless for a moment):
>Enlisted? In . . . in the army?

MOLLY (proudly):
>In the marines.

MRS. POWERS:
>But you won't go, will you, Tommy? Promise you won't go! You're just a baby!

TOM (awkwardly):
>Aw, Ma . . .

MRS. POWERS:
>If your pa was alive I wouldn't care so much. Promise, Tommy.

TOM:
>I won't go, Ma.

Mrs. Powers clings to him, weeping softly. Tom wants to get out of the situation.

TOM:
>When's he going?

MOLLY:
>As soon as he gets his call. He's up packing now.

Molly turns away with a little catch in her throat.

MRS. POWERS:

>Go up and see him, Tommy. (Bravely.) We . . . we ought to be proud of him.

Tom, anxious to escape the awkward situation, turns away and exits.

68. MIKE'S ROOM

It is a cheap bedroom, with two old-fashioned beds occupied by Tom and Mike. Mike has a valise on one of them and is packing away a few scanty clothes. He is so occupied that he doesn't notice Tom, who enters and stands just inside the door, still awkward.

TOM:

>'Lo, Mike.

MIKE (turns quickly):

>Oh, hello, Tom. Glad you came.

He assumes a rather important fatherly air toward Tom. Goes over and shakes hands with him.

MIKE:

>I suppose you heard?

TOM (nods):

>Gee, you're rushing it.

MIKE (seriously):

>Well, Tom, when our country needs us . . . she needs us.

He turns back and resumes his packing, very earnest and businesslike.

TOM:

>I suppose so. (Shifting uneasily from one foot to the other.) I suppose you think I ought to go too . . .

MIKE:

>No. (Goes over and lays his arm on Tom's shoulder in a big brother attitude.) Maybe it was selfish of

me, Tom, but one of us has got to stay and take care of Ma. You earn more than I do . . . and they'd have taken me first anyhow.

TOM:
You always did get all the breaks.

MIKE:
Don't look at it that way, Tom. You got to be the man of the family now. (Turns back to his packing.)

Mike watches him awkwardly for a moment.

MIKE (as he packs):
And while we're on the subject, . . . I wish you'd spend a little more time at home.

TOM (quick to take offense):
I gotta work, ain't I?

MIKE:
I understand that, but . . .

He becomes serious, like a teacher who has to correct one of his pupils. He walks over and shuts the door. Tom watches him with a slight scowl.

MIKE (coming back to Tom):
Listen, Tom, I was in a place today . . . and (embarrassed) I heard someone saying something.

TOM (on guard):
What of it?

MIKE (embarrassed):
Well . . . they were saying . . . well, it seemed like they were pointing a finger at you and Matt.

TOM (getting belligerent):
Who was? What rats was sayin' anything about me? I'll show 'em . . .

MIKE:
Now Tom . . .

TOM (in guilty anger):
> You're always hearing things. You'll get too much in your nose some day . . . and you'll wonder how you got it.

He thrusts his face close up to Mike's as he speaks.

MIKE:
> Well, for cryin' out loud! I heard a couple guys talkin' about you . . . as much as to say you were mixed up in some crooked work. What am I supposed to do . . . run?

TOM (slowly):
> Well . . . you ain't asking me. You're telling me . . . and I don't know nothin', see?

MIKE:
> All I got to say, Tom, is that you got a good job and you don't need these rats you're runnin' around with!

TOM (sneers):
> I suppose you want me to go to night school . . . and read poems. (Starts for the door.) I've heard some things myself.

MIKE (jumps after him and grabs his arm):
> There's nothin' to hear about me!

TOM (loftily):
> No? That's all you know. You ain't so smart. Books and that hooey don't hide everything.

MIKE:
> You're a liar, Tom! You're covering up.

TOM (wrenching his arm free):
> Covering up? To you? Say . . . you're only a sneak thief!

MIKE (aroused):
> What did you say?

TOM:

> You heard me . . . a sneak thief! A nickel snatcher! Robbin' the streetcar company . . .

Mike lashes out in blind fury and catches Tom on the chin, knocks him against the bed. Mike stands glowering over him. Tom gets up slowly; for once his overbearing, browbeating manner is conquered. Mike's glare plainly asks him if he wants any more. But Tom shows no intention of returning the blow. Mike with a scornful look on his face turns on his heel and walks out.

69.   MIKE'S ROOM   CLOSE-UP OF TOM

He glares after Mike malevolently, clenching his fist and gritting his teeth, furious at Mike but more furious at himself for having let Mike get away with it.

FADE OUT

TITLE: "The Eighteenth of January—The Eighteenth Hour—The Eighteenth Amendment."

FADE IN

70.   DOWNTOWN BUSINESS STREET   LONG SHOT   NIGHT

Sidewalks are crowded with pedestrians, the street crowded with traffic. Rich and poor carrying bundles, bottles, packages of all sizes. Many of them drunk and jostling against the others. Snatches of songs, such as "How Dry I Am," "We Won't Go Home till Morning."

LAP DISSOLVE TO:

71.   FRONT OF LIQUOR STORE

A long line of people pushing in one side of the door and beside them another line coming out, each one carrying a package of some kind. Many in evening clothes, others ragged. One of those coming out drops a bundle, which breaks. He mutters a curse and joins the empty-handed line going in.

LAP DISSOLVE TO:

72. CURB

Expensive limousine standing at the curb. A well-dressed man struggles up with his arms full of packages and bottles. A well-dressed woman reaches her arm out the limousine door. He thrusts the packages into her arms and hurries away for more. The packages are too much for the woman; she drops part of them into the gutter. She jumps out of the car and in spite of her expensive clothes tries to salvage what she can.

LAP DISSOLVE TO:

73. SIDEWALK

Crowds pushing in both directions with their arms full of packages, jostling one another, some of them cursing, others singing.

LAP DISSOLVE TO:

74. SIDEWALK

The pedestrian crowd jostling along. Through them comes a young couple, the man wheeling a baby carriage piled high with bottled goods, the woman carrying a six-months-old baby for whom there is no room in the baby carriage.

LAP DISSOLVE TO:

75. CURB

A florist wagon is backing up to the curb. The driver is throwing expensive flowers out of the wagon into the gutter ruthlessly to make room for packages which another man is loading in.

LAP DISSOLVE TO:

76. STREET

FULL SHOT of the orgy which outdoes any New Year's Eve or election night celebration.

FADE OUT

77. INT. EXPRESS OFFICE

The name of the express office is in reverse lettering on the window. Swanson, the general manager, is seated at his desk with Tom and Matt seated in chairs facing him. Swanson takes a box of cigars from his desk and in an expansive manner offers them to the boys. They take them, suspicious of what is coming. As Swanson hands out the cigars he is talking earnestly and in a very businesslike manner.

SWANSON:
> You see boys . . . this proposition . . . well, the government is going to let certain people, such as drugstores, handle the booze . . . and they got to get it from government warehouses and distilleries. Manufacturers of perfumes and hair tonics can also have it on a special permit. Now, someone has to haul this stuff and we've just landed the contract. It's the most important job we've got, and I'm going to give you boys a crack at it. It means a raise for both of you.

He smiles like a benign Santa Claus and looks the boys over expansively.

TOM (lighting his cigar):
> Why pick on us?

SWANSON (beaming):
> I was coming to that. It's because I'm proud to have you with us . . . proud because of your brother Mike.

78.   CLOSE SHOT ON TOM AND MATT
Tom turns to look at Matt with a sour expression as though asking "What does all this mean?"

SWANSON (voice off-scene):
> The record that boy Mike made over there in France would make anybody proud to say they had a member of his family with them. When I heard about the way he threw those hand grenades into that machine gun nest . . . boys, I wanted to get out and yell!

Tom turns back to face Swanson, puffing at his cigar and stolidly showing no other reaction to Swanson's enthusiasm. Matt shows a trifle more interest.

79.   INT. EXPRESS OFFICE   CLOSE SHOT ON THE GROUP

SWANSON (enthusiastic):
> It's all right for Congress to give them medals but such things should be recognized more substantially. So, I'm doing what little I can.

TOM (very matter of fact):
> You said something about a raise.

SWANSON:
> Sure, there's a raise, and part of that's on Mike's account too. Now that he's laid up in that war hospital in Washington, I figure a little extra money might be welcomed by the family. (Mischievously.) Hey?

Tom and Matt both nod in silence.

SWANSON (all business again):
> Now here . . .

He opens the drawer of the desk and takes out two pistols. He handles them as though he were afraid of them. The boys stare at them and then exchange glances.

SWANSON (pushing the revolver carefully across the desk toward the boys):
> Now, there'll be guys trying to hold you up . . . but I know they ain't going to get away with it. I've got permits for both of you to carry these. You . . . you're not afraid of them?

TOM (grimly):
> We'll try to get used to them.

SWANSON:
> All right. Then what do you say?

MATT:
> Do we haul just government booze?

SWANSON:
> Booze, alcohol, and wine . . . any kind of liquor that can be legally transported.

TOM (getting to his feet):
> When do we start?

SWANSON:
> As soon as the special truck is ready.

TOM:
> What do you say, Matt?

MATT (getting to his feet):
> All right with me.

Tom picks up the pistol, examines it with an expert eye. Matt does the same.

SWANSON (still afraid of the guns):
> I don't suppose you boys know anything about those things. But no doubt we can find someone to show you.

TOM (exchanging a quick look with Matt):
> We'll appreciate it.[10]

FADE OUT

80.　FADE IN

INT. PADDY'S OFFICE

Paddy is talking earnestly to Mike and Tom, who are listening with intent interest.

PADDY:
> You're a couple of fools to quit your jobs . . . you gotta better racket than you had before. Don't think booze ain't going to be valuable. I heard today that alcohol is going to thirty dollars a gallon. The real McCoy is hard to get. All you gotta do when you deliver a good shipment is to size up the layout and

let me know. I can take some of it and I know two
or three others who'll buy what I can't handle. It
means real dough . . . a three-way split . . . I said
the time would come when we could get together
. . . well, the time has come *now!*

As Paddy is talking we

FADE OUT

81. FADE IN
     EXT. DRUGSTORE   DAY
     The new specially built express truck is at the curb. Tom
     and Matt are unloading cases of whiskey. A crowd has
     gathered to watch the process, making wisecracks. Tom
     and Matt, who wear their pistols in holsters plainly
     visible, are enjoying the attention they receive. Voices
     from the crowd are heard: "Boy! Look at that booze,"
     "Give us a drink, son," "Where'd you get it, big boy?!"

82. CLOSE SHOT ON TOM AND MATT
     as they each pick up a case. They carry themselves in a
     lofty manner, pretending to ignore the crowd, but are
     plainly pleased at being the center of so much interest.

     VOICE (off-scene):
         If we rush those guys we'll have booze for six
         months.

     ANOTHER VOICE (off-scene):
         Yeah . . . but look at those gats!

     Tom and Matt start into the store, each with a case of
     whiskey.

                                            LAP DISSOLVE TO:

83. BACK ROOM OF DRUGSTORE
     Ten cases of whiskey are stacked up underneath the
     window in a typical drugstore back room, and Tom and
     Matt are just placing two more on top of the pile. One
     of the cases near the bottom has broken open and the
     bottle is visible.

TOM:
> That's all.

He starts away. Matt stops and reaches down to the broken case, is about to pick up a bottle and put it under his jacket. Tom catches him by the arm:

TOM:
> What do you want to swipe our own stuff for?

MATT:
> *Our* stuff!

TOM (in low voice):
> It will be.

MATT (suddenly understanding):
> That's right. (Turns to survey the cases gloatingly.) The whole ten cases.

TOM (as he puts the bottle back into the broken case):
> Twelve. The guy had two already.

Matt grins and nods. Tom suddenly changes his mind, turns, and puts the bottle on the prescription desk behind him. Matt stares at him.

MATT:
> What the . . .

TOM:
> Aw, what's one bottle. The poor stiff'll need a drink in the morning when he finds everything gone.

FADE OUT

84.   FADE IN

INT. PADDY'S BACK ROOM

This is the room where drinks are served at tables entered by the old family entrance. Paddy, Tom, and Matt are seated at one of the tables. Ernie, the bartender, comes in with drinks on a tray. Paddy is just finishing making three piles of bills. He shoves one across to Tom and one to Matt.

PADDY:
> There, are you satisfied?

MATT (picks up his pile of money almost in a daze):
> *I'll* say.

Tom also picks up his and fingers it as though he were afraid of it.

PADDY:
> Pretty soft, wasn't it? How'd ya like playing with Paddy?

TOM:
> I don't know what to do with so much coin.

PADDY:
> You ain't started. I'll make big shots out of ya yet.

TOM (enthusiastically):
> Anything ya say goes with me, Paddy.

MATT (enthusiastically):
> And me too.

PADDY (picks up a drink):
> Then here's to us.[11] (They drink.) Now, what else do you know?

TOM (putting down his glass):
> Well . . . we hauled some stuff out of a G. warehouse this morning. There was a load of bonded stuff . . . more than a hundred barrels I counted.

PADDY (excitedly):
> What's that?

TOM:
> But it's on the top floor. There's no way to get it out.

PADDY (excitedly):
> No way to get it out? (Picks up a pencil and begins rapidly figuring.) Do you know what a hundred barrels are worth? (Figures.) More than a hundred and fifty grand! We *gotta* get it out!

Tom and Matt gasp. Their lips form the words a hundred and fifty grand.

TOM:

> I didn't know there was that much dough in the world.

FADE OUT

FADE IN

85.   EXT. BONDED WAREHOUSE   DAY

A LONG SHOT to establish the warehouse adjoining an open air gasoline filling station, which occupies the street corner. The open space should run right up to the dead wall of the warehouse. The building itself should have windows high up in the wall and across the top the sign U.S. Bonded Warehouse #114.

The usual traffic of cars is stopping at the filling station, which has a Negro attendant.

86.   ALLEY AT THE BACK OF THE WAREHOUSE

Shoot so as to pick up the sign from another angle and establish it as the same building. Dutch Sieberling and Bugs Healey, dressed as telephone linemen, are just starting to climb a telegraph pole, which stands at the corner of the warehouse, running up so that a window is near the top of the pole.

They carry the usual lineman's tools, and in addition have a coiled-up hose. One of them also has a bicycle tire pump sticking out of his hip pocket. As they start to climb, the uniformed policeman comes down the alley. He stops and looks and watches them a second. They continue climbing, ignoring him.

POLICEMAN:

> What's wrong, boys?

BUGS:

> Broken wire. What do you think, we're doing this for exercise?

Policeman nods, goes on down the alley. Bugs and Dutch resume their climb.

LAP DISSOLVE TO:

87. INT. WAREHOUSE   MED. LONG SHOT OF THE UPPER FLOOR
It is half filled with whiskey barrels standing on end. The window is open and Bugs and Dutch are climbing in from the telephone pole, dragging in the hose after them. They work very fast, as though on a careful plan.

88. FILLING STATION
A large gasoline tank truck, evidently new, drives in, comes up alongside the warehouse, and stops. Tom is driving, Matt seated beside him.

89. CLOSE SHOT ON TOM AND MATT
in the driver's seat of the tank truck, keeping an alert lookout on all sides. They light cigarettes and pretend to be unconcerned.

90. INT. WAREHOUSE
Dutch and Bugs have one of the casks on its side. The bung is out and the hose thrust into the bunghole. One of them drops the other end of the hose out of the window while the other stands by with a bicycle pump to start the siphon suction going.

91. FILLING STATION   CLOSE SHOT ON THE TRUCK
The end of the hose and a small piece of rope are dropped down the side of the building. Matt is on the ground and has the filling port of the tank open. He immediately grabs the end of the hose and sticks it into the filling port.

TOM (in eager whisper):
    Grab the rope! One jerk to start . . . two to stop!

Matt immediately seizes the rope and jerks it, then walks away casually with his hands in his pocket, walking around the truck unconcerned, but keeping a sharp lookout. In a second we hear the sound of liquid pouring into the tank.

92. INT. WAREHOUSE
Bugs is standing by the barrel which has the hose in the bung. Dutch is rolling up another barrel, taking out the bung.

LAP DISSOLVE TO:

93. FILLING STATION   CLOSE SHOT ON THE TANK TRUCK
Matt comes along the side, makes a quick examination, signals to Tom that it's about full. Tom nods and pantomimes for him to jerk the rope twice. Matt gives the rope two jerks, waits a second, then removes the hose, leaves it dangling on the wall of the building still dripping. He closes the port quickly, gets in beside Tom, and they drive off.

94. ALLEY
The uniformed policeman is strolling down the alley, chatting with a plainclothes cop. At the distance we do not hear their words. Plainclothesman is biting off the end of a cigar. As they turn the corner of the warehouse Tom and Matt with their truck drive in and pass them. Tom and Matt keep an alert eye on the two cops, but the latter merely give a glance at the truck and pass on along the wall of the warehouse.

95. FILLING STATION   CLOSE SHOT ON THE TWO COPS
walking along the side of the warehouse. Plainclothesman feeling in his pocket for matches. PAN with them as they stroll along. They come to where the hose is dangling against the wall. A few drops of whiskey are dripping from the end of it and splashing on the wall.

Neither of the cops see it, but as they pass, the plainclothesman scratches a match on the wall. Immediately the whiskey on the wall takes fire and the flame runs up the wall to the end of the hose. Both of the policemen jump back in amazement.

INSERT   CLOSE-UP OF THE END OF THE HOSE with the flame running up the wall to the end of the hose and burning out. The whiskey begins to drip again in small drops.

96.   FILLING STATION   CLOSE SHOT ON TWO COPS
They stare at the wall and at each other. Plainclothesman goes up to the hose and sniffs it.

PLAINCLOTHESMAN:
    Smells like whiskey! (He puts his tongue to the end of the hose.) Tastes like whiskey! (He hands the hose to the uniformed cop, who tastes it.)

UNIFORMED COP:
    It *is* whiskey!

They glance up to see where the hose is coming from. Plainclothesman takes ahold of the rope and pulls it as though to see where it is fastened. Immediately a stream of whiskey starts pouring out of the hose. They jump back amazed.

PLAINCLOTHESMAN:
    It's a hoist! Turn in the alarm!

The two policemen run out in opposite directions. As they go, the Negro station attendant comes in, stares bug-eyed at the stream of whiskey, sniffs, then suddenly going into action, he turns and runs for the filling station.

97.   FILLING STATION   A CLOSE SHOT BEHIND THE BUILDING
Four Negroes squatting on the ground at a crap game.

NEGRO (rolling the dice):
    C'mon you big Richard. (His face lights up as he sees the dice.) Do you all see what I sees?

ANOTHER NEGRO (who has raised his head and is sniffing):
   Does you all smell what I smells?

The other Negroes raise their heads and sniff.

THIRD NEGRO:
   Once upon a time, ah used to know that smell.

They all get to their feet, look around to locate the direction of the smell, and rush out leaving the dice and money on the ground.

98.   FILLING STATION   CLOSE SHOT AT THE HOSE
A full stream is pouring out of it, and the Negro attendant is rapidly filling a can. He has oil cans and gasoline cans of all sizes on the ground beside him and is filling up furiously. The crap shooters rush in. They push the attendant aside and squabble over the hose, drinking from the end of it eagerly, splashing the liquor all over as they push one another aside for a turn, with shouts of glee.[12]

                                                    FADE OUT

      FADE IN
99.   INT. TAILOR SHOP   DAY
Tom with his coat and vest off is being measured by a tailor. He calls off the measurements and an assistant repeats them as he marks them down on his card. Mirrors in the background and a couple of tables piled with bolts of woolens at the side. Matt is standing by these, fingering the materials awkwardly, while another tailor is telling about the weave, etc. The whole thing is new to Matt and Tom, and they are awkward about the whole thing, Tom watching the tailor suspiciously as he passes the tape around him.

TAILOR (measuring Tom's waistband):
   Thirty-one and a half.[13]

ASSISTANT (repeats):
> Thirty-one and a half.

TOM (putting his thumb inside the waistband in the spot where he carries his gun):
> Give me plenty of room there, fellow.

TAILOR (feeling timidly of Tom's biceps):
> Ah, gentleman, here is where you need the room. (Admiringly.) Such a muscle.

TOM:
> Make this snappy . . . or you'll see what that's good for.

MATT (coming over):
> Yeah, let's get out of here.

TAILOR (hastily):
> Sure . . . sure. (Measuring.) Forty-six and a quarter.

ASSISTANT (repeating):
> Forty-six and a quarter.

TAILOR:
> Did you read about that big robbery at the booze warehouse? (Measuring.) Thirty-two and a half.

ASSISTANT (repeats):
> Thirty-two and a half.

TAILOR:
> . . . right under their noses? Hey?

TOM (with a quick glance at Matt):
> A fellow told me about it.

TAILOR (measuring):
> Twenty-two.

ASSISTANT (repeats):
> Twenty-two.

TAILOR (measuring as he talks):
    If them birds get away, they'll be rich for life . . .
    twenty-seven and a half.

ASSISTANT (repeating):
    Twenty-seven and a half.

TAILOR:
    Did you see what the papers said? (In awestricken
    voice.) Hundred fifty thousand!

ASSISTANT (repeating):
    Hundred and fifty thousand . . .

He is about to write when he realizes there is some mis-
take. He gazes up at Tom open-mouthed, then realizes
it is an error and starts erasing the last note.

TOM (impatiently):
    How long is this going to last?

TAILOR (hastily):
    All through now, gentlemen. Thank you, thank
    you.

TOM (putting on his coat and vest):
    And remember what I told you about that— (he
    puts his thumb in his waistline again) belt.

MATT:
    And listen— (pointing to his sleeve) don't forget—
    six buttons.

TOM (pantomiming, drawing his sleeve across his nose):
    Be careful, Matt, or you're going to cut your nose
    right off of ya.

The tailor laughs obsequiously at the joke, as Tom resumes putting on his coat.

FADE OUT

FADE IN

100.   EXT. BLACK AND TAN CAFE   NIGHT

The outside of a typical black and tan cafe, mixed groups milling, passing, and loitering on the sidewalk. Considerable automobile traffic and general activity. Cars parked at the curb.

Tom and Matt drive up in a shiny new car, have difficulty in finding a place to park at the curb.

101.   EXT. BLACK AND TAN CAFE   CLOSE SHOT ON THE NEW CAR

It is bright and spotless. Matt and Tom get out. They are dressed in new perfectly tailored suits, have new stylish hats and gloves. It is the first time we have seen them wearing hats. They look like prosperity itself, and they carry themselves with a new air.

The doorman hurries out to meet them. Matt turns back to look at the car, takes his handkerchief and wipes a spot of dust off the fender, surveys the car proudly.

DOORMAN:
    Well, well . . . if it ain't Mr. Tom and Mr. Matt.

He signals the attendant who comes over and gets into the car as he speaks.

TOM:
    Hello, George. How's business?

DOORMAN:
    Big night.

The attendant starts to drive the car off but clashes the gears.

TOM (turning suddenly):
    Hey there, stupe! That's no Ford . . . It's got gears.

They watch the attendant, see that he handles the car properly, then turn again toward cafe.

102.   EXT. CAFE   CLOSE SHOT AT THE ENTRANCE
At one side of the door is an old Negress squatted on
the pavement selling bouquets. On the other side of the
door is a Negro couple in a hot argument. Tom and Matt
enter. The old Negress extends a gaudy bouquet to Tom
who takes it, hands it to Matt. Matt is watching the Negro couple and takes the bouquet unconsciously. Then
Matt notices the bouquet in his hand, throws it at the
Negress, scattering her whole stock. The old woman begins to protest. Tom takes a bill out of his pocket and
throws it at her. She quiets down immediately. The boys
disappear into the cafe.[14]

103.   INT. BLACK AND TAN CAFE
A large room, tables surrounding a dance floor, dim
lights, and an air of heaviness. A Negro orchestra on a
raised platform. Negro waiters are entertainers. The
tables have no cloths. Some of them are occupied by
white parties, others by blacks. Floor is fairly well filled
with dancers, both black and white, but in no case do
we show the whites dancing or mixing with the blacks.
    Tom and Matt enter and stand looking over the room
for a second. Headwaiter rushes up and greets them.

HEADWAITER:
    Ah, Mr. Powers . . . Mr. Doyle. Alone as usual?

TOM:
    I am. Matt's all fixed up . . . he's got me with him.

HEADWAITER (as he leads them off toward the table):
    The night's young yet. You'll wind up with some-
    thing.

MATT:
    Yeah . . . with a morning paper.

He stops, nudges Tom, and indicates the table near the
dance floor.

104. INT. BLACK AND TAN CAFE   CLOSE SHOT ON ONE OF THE
      TABLES

Kitty and Mamie, girls about Tom's age, who look like regular patrons of the place, are at the table with two men who have passed out. One of them is slumped down in the chair and the other is asleep with his head on his folded arms leaning across the table.[15]

Waiter is standing at the table and Kitty is pushing an empty glass toward him, pantomiming she wants another drink. The waiter looks toward the two souses doubtfully, doesn't know whether he's going to get his pay. He goes over to the one whose head is on the table, pries open his hand, sees there is a bill in it, takes out the bill, nods to Kitty, picks up the glass, and exits.

During this time, Mamie has been looking around the room and she has caught Matt's eye. She is interested. She nods, gets up, walks toward the dance floor.

105. INT. BLACK AND TAN CAFE   CLOSE-UP AT THE EDGE OF
      THE DANCE FLOOR

Mamie meets Matt. Without a word they dance off together.

106. INT. BLACK AND TAN CAFE   CLOSE SHOT ON TOM AND
      THE HEADWAITER

The headwaiter indicates seats at a vacant table. Tom is watching Matt and Mamie, then turns his attention to Kitty and the two souses.

TOM:
    Why don't you send them smack-offs home to their mothers? They ain't any good to the joint anymore.

HEADWAITER (with a grin):
    And the ladies too?

TOM (hitting him playfully on the arm):
    Don't be sill'.

The headwaiter grins understandingly, nods, turns away with a signal.

107.   INT. BLACK AND TAN CAFE   CLOSE SHOT ON MATT AND
       MAMIE

among the dancers. They are silent; so far they haven't spoken a word to each other. The music stops, the dancers begin to leave the floor.

MATT:
   How about something with ice in it?

MAMIE (hesitates):
   Why . . . we're with a couple of friends . . .

Matt turns away and looks toward the table.

MATT:
   I know it. I'm one of them.

108.   INT. BLACK AND TAN CAFE   CLOSE SHOT ON KITTY'S
       TABLE

Two big bouncers are helping the two souses out of their chairs, marching them off toward the door. The souses are too far gone to protest. As soon as they are out of the way, Tom slips into the chair beside Kitty.

TOM:
   Hello, babe. What are ya going to have?

KITTY (looks Tom over quickly with approval):
   Whatever you say, big boy.

TOM:
   You're a swell dish . . . I think I'm going to adopt you.

Waiter bustles in, arranging the new setups. Matt and Mamie return to the table.

MATT (indicating Mamie):
   Look what I got measured for, Tom.

TOM (waving Matt away and devoting his attention to Kitty):
   I don't even know you're here.

Matt grins and he and Mamie seat themselves at the table. Tom signals for a waiter.

FADE OUT

FADE IN

109.   INT. PADDY'S BACK ROOM   DAY

Paddy is seated talking to Leeman at a table, on which there are a bottle and glasses. Leeman is a very prosperous-looking man, well past middle age, reticent, cautious, suggests the retired capitalist.

His hand rests on the head of an ivory cane while he sits talking to Paddy.

PADDY:
  Then it's a deal?

LEEMAN (guardedly):
  If you can assure me my name will be . . . ah . . . protected.

As they are talking, Tom and Matt enter. They are dressed in their express driver clothes, wear caps.

PADDY (to Leeman):
  You'll be protected all over the place. (To Tom and Matt.) 'Lo, boys. You can take those clothes off. You got new jobs.

TOM:
  Yeah?

PADDY:
  Yeah. First, meet Mr. Leeman. These are the two lads I've been telling you about.

Leeman shakes hands with them in very dignified manner.

PADDY (continues):
  Sit down, boys. How do you like the brewery business?

MATT (taking a chair):
  Don't know nothing about it.

PADDY:

You will. You're in it now. Mr. Leeman and I have got it all fixed. You see, Mr. Leeman owns that big brewery over on Union Avenue . . .

TOM:

That's been closed ever since . . .

PADDY:

Yeah . . . but it's going to open up. (Ironically.) You see, I've discovered that the working man is demanding his beer (with a wink) and so we've answered the call of public duty.

LEEMAN (hastily):

Mr. Ryan has assured me, gentlemen, that I am to do nothing except furnish the facilities . . .

PADDY:

All k.o., Mr. Leeman. You make the beer . . . that's easy. We distribute it . . . that's tougher. Some of those speakies around here may not want to take our stuff. There's a mob on the North Side that's been selling 'em, and they ain't going to exactly kiss us when they learn that this is *our* territory.

LEEMAN (with pretended timidity):

I . . . I hope . . . there'll be no violence.

PADDY:

Violence? Oh no! Tom and Matt here, I'll just go down and read them a few poems.[16]

LEEMAN:

You spoke of a rather remarkable man from the West Side.

PADDY:

Yeah, Nails Nathan . . .

TOM (almost gasps):

Jeez, Paddy, is Nails Nathan puttin' in with us?

PADDY:
> Be here any minute.

MATT (gasps):
> Whew!

LEEMAN:
> I don't believe I'm acquainted with the gentleman . . .

PADDY:
> Then you're the only man in town that ain't. At least everybody's heard of him . . . hey, boys? (Tom and Matt nod eagerly.) Believe me, Mr. Leeman, when Nails Nathan and his mob start on a job, it's already done. And if this Schemer Burns crowd tries to muscle in on us . . . well, I pity 'em!

LEEMAN:
> You understand, of course, that my desire is merely to furnish a better grade of beer than the working man can now obtain under the present . . . ah . . . unfortunate . . .

NAILS (voice off-scene):
> In your hat!

They all turn startled in the direction of the voice.

110. INT. PADDY'S BACK ROOM   CLOSE SHOT ON NAILS
He is just coming through from the swinging doors of the bar. He is dressed in the height of fashion, the latest in hat and overcoat, gloves, and a cane. Carries himself with a jaunty manner and with supreme self-confidence.

NAILS:
> And again, in your hat! I've heard that north wind blow before. If you're in this, you're in for the coin, same as the rest of us.

He advances toward the table.

111.   INT. PADDY'S BACK ROOM   MED. SHOT AT THE TABLE
Paddy, Leeman, Matt, and Tom are standing facing
Nails as he walks jauntily into the SHOT. Tom and Matt
are scowling. Tom steps forward as though resenting
the intrusion of this fresh person.

PADDY:

Gentlemen, this is Mr. Nails Nathan.

Tom and Matt give another gasp of surprise.

NAILS:

Born "Samuel" . . . (extending his hand to Tom)
and you're Tom Powers. Glad to know ya.

Tom gives a gasp of amazement as he shakes Nails's
hand.

NAILS:

. . . and you're Matt. (Nails grasps Matt's hand.)

TOM (amazed):

How . . . how did you know . . . ?

NAILS (breezily):

Know all about you. Paddy's been talking.

PADDY:

Meet Mr. Leeman, Nails.

NAILS:

Tickled pink. (Shakes hands with Leeman.) Don't
take offense at anything I say, Mr. Leeman. But if
we're in the racket together, we've got to take the
cheaters off!

LEEMAN (hastily):

My . . . my name is not to appear . . .

NAILS (breezily):

We won't use it in our advertising. (To Paddy.) Well,
Paddy . . . the mob will be all set by the time you
can open. Got some routes laid out, and the stock's
all marked.

LEEMAN (greedily):
> You mean, you have customers all signed up?

PADDY (laughs):
> Signed up? Tom and Matt'll attend to that. They'll be the trouble squad.

NAILS:
> And if they need help . . . well, Nails has some handy boys with their gloves all oiled.

LEEMAN (with pretended alarm):
> Dear me, I'm afraid this means . . .

PADDY (he is suddenly tense and menacing; he leans forward with a clenched fist on the table):
> It means, they buy our beer, or they don't buy *any* beer!

He looks at Nails, Tom, and Matt for confirmation and they nod.

FADE OUT

FADE IN

112. INT. BREWERY YARD   FULL SHOT   DAY
> A truck is at the loading platform almost completely loaded with beer kegs, which are covered with a tarpaulin. Couple more trucks waiting for entrance to the platform.
>
> Matt and Tom with their new car waiting to follow the first car out. Nails Nathan running up and down the platform giving instructions and showing Dutch Sieberling how to load his truck. Nails is still dressed in his immaculate clothes but has his coat and vest off exhibiting a fancy silk shirt.

113. CLOSE SHOT AT THE LOADING PLATFORM

NAILS (to Dutch on truck):
> Now get going! And listen . . . Don't take any backtalk from these speakies, just tell 'em, here's the

beer they ordered. If they doubt it, call on Tom and Matt . . .

Dutch climbs into the cab of the truck, starts it up.

NAILS (calling off):
     All right, Tom . . . Matt, get going!

114.   INT. BREWERY YARD   CLOSE SHOT ON TOM AND MATT IN
     THEIR CAR
     Matt driving, Tom sitting beside him. They signal okay to Nails and start up.

115.   INT. BREWERY YARD   CLOSE SHOT AT THE GATE
     Hack Miller as watchman opens the gate and allows Dutch's truck to pass out. It is followed by Tom and Matt in their car.

                                        FADE OUT

     FADE IN
116.   INT. SPEAKEASY   FULL SHOT
     Place resembles an old-time saloon with bar along one side, sawdust on the floor, two or three tables and chairs in the room.
         Steve, the proprietor, is behind the bar serving a customer. Tom and Matt stride in and go up to the bar. Steve nods at them guardedly. He suspects trouble with them.

TOM:
     Hello, Steve. How's business?

STEVE:
     Business? There ain't such a thing.

Dutch enters behind them and stands in the door expectantly.

MATT:
     Dutch was telling us that you only took two kegs of beer the last trip and now you don't want any at all.

STEVE:
> Business is on the bum.

TOM:
> Give us a couple beers . . . that'll help out a little.

Steve draws the beer, casting furtive glances at the two men at the table. Tom takes a drink of his beer, then spits it out on the bar with an expression of disgust.

TOM:
> This ain't *our* beer!

MATT:
> Where'd you get this swill?

STEVE:
> It's good, ain't it? And it's cheaper than yours.

TOM (to one of the customers):
> What are you paying for it?

CUSTOMER:
> Two bits a glass.

TOM (to Steve):
> I thought so. You can sell ours for the same price.

Tom walks around the end of the bar, goes behind it. Steve backs away alarmed.

117. INT. SPEAKEASY   CLOSE-UP
of the row of faucets behind the bar. Tom's hand reaches in and turns each one of the faucets wide open so that a stream of beer runs from each down on the floor.

118. INT. SPEAKEASY   CLOSE SHOT
on Tom and Steve with Matt on the other side of the bar. Steve makes a move as though to shut off the faucet. Tom glares at him menacingly.

TOM:
> Keep your hands off! Someone's got to protect your customers!

Steve gets the menace in Tom's glance and backs away.

119.   INT. SPEAKEASY   CLOSE-UP
of the beer splashing on the floor from the faucets and running away in a stream.

120.   INT. SPEAKEASY   CLOSE SHOT
on Tom, Matt, and Steve. The beer still running.

STEVE:
But what am I going to do? I can't help it if I have to buy from Schemer Burns. They tell me the same thing you do!

TOM (steps up to Steve and slaps his face with his open hand):
You're yellow!

Tom grabs Steve by coat front, ready to slug him.

STEVE:
Please, you . . . you ain't going to slug me, are you?

TOM:
Maybe not . . . today. But I'm tellin' you this for the last time. When Dutch comes around, he's going to leave you some beer, and you're going to take it . . . and cough up with the coin. If you don't somebody'll be droppin' by here and pick your teeth out! Get me?

Steve nods, turns to look at the faucets. Dutch stands in doorway.

TOM:
And you'll be needin' some right away. How much shall we leave?

STEVE (stammering):
T-t-two kegs . . .

TOM (to Dutch):
> You hear that, Dutch? Bring in five kegs.

Dutch grins, nods, and exits.

FADE OUT

FADE IN

121.   POWERS LIVING ROOM   CLOSE SHOT
of an elaborate floral piece with the wording Welcome Home Michael Powers.

122.   POWERS LIVING ROOM   CLOSE SHOT
on Molly. Elaborate floral pieces of all kinds are banked against the wall and Molly is passing along them reading the cards. We PAN with her as she walks along.

MOLLY (reading):
> Mr. and Mrs. Patrick J. Ryan, Mr. and Mrs. Bernard Grogan, Mr. John Healey . . .

We PAN with her as she reaches the big welcome piece. She looks at the card.

MOLLY (reading):
> Mr. Samuel Nathan. (Turns to look off at Mike off-scene, in surprise.)

123.   INT. POWERS LIVING ROOM   CLOSE SHOT
on Mike with officer Pat Burke sitting beside him. Mike is in his uniform and his chest is covered with medals and decorations. He is propped up on the chair, looks very pale and weak.

MIKE:
> Samuel Nathan? I never heard of him.

PAT:
> Nails Nathan . . . one of Tom's . . . new friends.

Pat speaks with a suggestion of aversion in his voice and Mike looks at him quickly, suspiciously.

MIKE:
> What's Tom doing now, Pat? Mother said something about a political job . . .

PAT (he is troubled; looks around the room as though to be sure no one is in hearing):
> Well, (hesitates) I might as well tell you what I hear . . . [17]

He hitches his chair closer to Mike and begins to speak in low voice which we do not hear.

124.   POWERS DINING ROOM
Table has been set for six people and is profusely decorated with flowers. Mrs. Powers and Mrs. Doyle are bustling about, making final arrangements. Tom and Matt dressed in their finest clothes are propping a keg of beer up in the middle of the table. It has a spigot already fixed.

MRS. POWERS:
> That's nice of you, Tommy. But I don't believe Mike'll be able to drink any.

TOM:
> It's the best beer in town . . . do him good.

125.   POWERS LIVING ROOM   CLOSE SHOT ON MIKE AND PAT
Pat still talking in low voice to Mike. He is greatly troubled. Mike is staring straight ahead of him with indignation growing in him. Mrs. Powers enters and Pat immediately straightens up, gives Mike a signal to indicate that Mrs. Powers doesn't know anything about this and they mustn't discuss it in her presence.

MRS. POWERS:
> Dinner's all ready, Michael. Shall I help you in?

MIKE:
> No, Mother. I can make it.

Pat gets up and helps Mike to his feet.

PAT:
> I'll be running along. See you all later.

As Mike and his mother start for the dining room, we
LAP DISSOLVE TO:

126. POWERS DINING ROOM
The dinner is near its finish. We come in on a CLOSE SHOT of Mike seated at the head of the table. He is silent, staring at the keg of beer in the middle of the table with a sort of suppressed fury beginning to show in his face. PAN DOWN the table, pick up Tom and Matt seated at one side of the table eating voraciously.

Molly and Mrs. Doyle opposite them and Mrs. Powers are at the foot of the table watching Mike with a worried expression.

MRS. POWERS:
> How's the meat, Michael?

127. POWERS DINING ROOM   CLOSE-UP OF MIKE
He doesn't reply for a moment, evidently occupied with bitter thoughts.

MIKE (suddenly coming to himself):
> Fine, Ma.

MRS. POWERS (off-scene):
> I wish you'd eat more. Try some of the sauerkraut.[18]

MIKE:
> I've had plenty, Ma.

He relapses into his preoccupation.

128. POWERS DINING ROOM   CLOSE SHOT ON THE TABLE

MOLLY:
> Tell Matt and Tom about the medals.

MATT:
> Yeah . . . how about 'em, Mike?

MIKE (bringing his attention to the conversation with difficulty):
> That'll keep till later.

129. POWERS DINING ROOM   CLOSE SHOT ON TOM AND MATT
Tom looks up at Mike curiously, then at Matt, as though asking what's the matter with him. Matt gets to his feet, picks up some glasses, and starts filling them at the spigot.

MATT:
> Say! We haven't drunk to your health! This is a swell celebration!

PAN with him as he carries a glass of beer over and puts it in front of Mike. Mike stares at it as though it were something foul. Matt doesn't notice his manner but distributes other glasses down the table. PAN with him until he has gone clear around the table. Then he stands by his chair and raises his glass:

MATT:
> Here's to you, Mike!

He drinks his beer.

130. POWERS DINING ROOM   CLOSE-UP ON MIKE
He sits staring at the beer, tapping the table nervously with his fingers, evidently on the verge of an outbreak.

MATT (off-scene):
> Why don't you drink, Mike? (Pause.) C'mon . . . it's only beer.

MIKE (tensely):
> I don't want any, Matt.

131. POWERS DINING ROOM   FULL SHOT ON THE GROUP

TOM (annoyed at Mike's attitude):
> I suppose beer ain't good enough for you since you had all that wine over there.

MRS. POWERS (gets up, walks toward Mike):
Go on and drink a glass, Michael. It'll give you
strength. (She picks up the glass and hands it to
him.)

MIKE (taking the glass from her and replacing it on the
table):
No, Ma . . . I don't think I will.[19]

TOM (fiercely):
What the dickens is eating you?

MIKE (turning on Tom with a glare of cold fury):
Say . . . I ain't interfering with your drinking. If
you want to drink it, go on. But if I don't want to,
I don't have to. (He speaks as though under a great
strain.)

TOM (sneering):
So beer ain't good enough for you?

Mike is silent for a moment, then he jumps to his feet
in fury.

MIKE:
You think I'd care if it was just beer in that keg?
(Raising his voice to a shout.) I know what's in it! I
know what you've been doing all this time . . .
where you got those clothes and those new cars!
You've been telling Ma that you've gone into politics . . . that you're on the city payroll! Pat Burke
told me everything! (Looks wildly from Tom to
Matt.) *You murderers!* It's not beer in that keg! It's
beer and *blood! Blood of men!*

He dashes to the side of the table, seizes the keg, and
heaves it onto the floor with a crash. The women
scream. Matt looks on stupidly. Tom turns away with a
sneer of contempt as Mike collapses into a chair. He
starts out but stops in the doorway and turns back.

TOM:
> You ain't changed a bit. And say . . . you ain't so
> good yourself![20] You killed . . . and you liked it! You
> didn't get them medals for holding hands with
> them Germans.

MRS. POWERS (coming over quickly to Tom):
> Don't, Tommy boy! He ain't himself. Don't get him
> excited. This trip was too much for the poor soul.
> Lord have pity on him . . . he's been through too
> much. Please, Tommy . . .

TOM (to Matt):
> C'mon, Matt. Let's get out of here. You can send
> my clothes to the Washington Arms Hotel!

MRS. POWERS (trying to hold Tom):
> Don't be angry, Tommy. Don't go away.

Tom shakes her hand off his arm, turns away. Matt follows, leaving Mrs. Powers watching them with a look
of bitter disappointment.

132. POWERS DINING ROOM   CLOSE SHOT OF MIKE
sitting in the chair glowering across the table at nothing.

FADE OUT

FADE IN

133. MATT'S BEDROOM   DAY
A small bedroom with the usual furnishings found in a
moderate-priced flat. Matt dressed only in his pajamas
is sitting up in bed as Mamie enters with a tray of breakfast. Mamie in attractive house negligee. Mamie ar-
ranges the tray on a small table and starts to push it up
to the side of the bed. She is happy, humming a tune to
herself.

MAMIE:
> Time to get up, lazy bones. Going to sleep all day?

MATT (pretending to be severe):
> Aw, button up. I'm to kip as long as I like.

MAMIE (pretending to be offended):
> Why Matt Doyle, the way you talk to me . . . and
> after I cooked this lovely breakfast . . . with my
> own hands.

MATT (seizes her playfully and forces her down onto the
bed beside him):
> If it's as good as all that, I'll split it with you.

MAMIE (struggling to free herself):
> If you don't let me go . . . I'll never speak to you
> again.

MATT:
> You talk too much anyhow.

Mamie struggles playfully to release herself but Matt
holds her tight, rubbing his chin against her cheek.

MAMIE (pushing his face away playfully, feeling of her
own cheek):
> At least you might get a shave.

Matt seizes her again, rubbing his rough chin against
her cheek. Phone rings off-scene.

MAMIE (struggling):
> There . . . let me go. The phone!

MATT:
> Let Kitty answer it.

He holds one arm firmly around her, picks up a piece of
toast from the tray, and starts stuffing it into her mouth,
Mamie all the time struggling playfully.

134. APARTMENT LIVING ROOM
Kitty, also in an attractive house negligee, is at the
phone.

KITTY (in phone):
> Who?[21] (Greatly impressed.) Oh . . . just a minute.
> (Turns and calls off.) Tom! It's for you.

127

TOM (voice off-scene surly and sleepy):
Who is it?

KITTY:
Nails Nathan.

She leaves the receiver off the hook and starts out. Just
as she reaches the door Tom enters, just finishing putting a dressing gown over his pajamas. His hair is tou-
sled and his eyes half shut. Kitty looks at him a little
askance. The attitude of both indicates that there has
been a quarrel going on. Tom ignores her and stumbles
over toward the phone.

KITTY:
Your food will be waiting for you when you get
through.

Tom doesn't answer, picks up the phone.

TOM (in phone):
Hello, Nails . . . Yeah. Not so good. Naw. Oh
nothin' . . . just this jane gettin' on my nerves . . .

135.   TELEPHONE BOOTH   CLOSE SHOT OF NAILS AT THE PHONE
He is spick-and-span in a very correct riding habit, carries a hunting crop, and bears himself even more jauntily than usual.

NAILS (in telephone):
Listen . . . I'm fed up on these rubber checks
bouncin' in. We're layin' down good beer and gettin' a lotta bum paper. I got one here for twelve
hundred from that Pete over on Kedzie. Get over
there. I want the dough . . . cash or his heart. Bring
in one or the other . . .

136.   APARTMENT LIVING ROOM   CLOSE SHOT OF TOM AT THE
PHONE LISTENING

TOM (into telephone):
> I'll bring you both! (Laughs.) Leave it to me, Nails. (Hangs up receiver and turns to call off.) Matt, shake a leg. Nails wants us.

MATT (off-scene):
> Right with you.

Tom rubs his eyes, stumbles out of the room.

137. **BREAKFAST NOOK**
The usual two-seated affair off the kitchen. Kitty is bustling about the table, on which she has laid out breakfast. Tom enters.

KITTY (brightly):
> All ready, Tom.

TOM (surly):
> Nuts to that stuff. Ain't you got a drink in the house?

KITTY:
> Not before breakfast, Tom.

TOM:
> I didn't ask for any lip! I asked for a drink!

KITTY:
> Yes, Tom. But I wish . . . (Turns away to get the drink.)

TOM:
> You're always wishin'. You got the gimmes for fair! I'm going to get you a bag of peanuts![22]

Kitty comes back, has very serious expression on her face.

KITTY:
> Maybe you got someone you like better.

Tom stares at her ferociously for a second, then reaches

over on the table, picks up a half grapefruit, throws it at Kitty's face, and strides out. Kitty sinks down into one of the seats at the table, stares after him brokenhearted.

138. MATT'S BEDROOM
Matt and Mamie side by side on the bed finishing breakfast. Tom enters.

TOM (sourly):
C'mon, Matt . . . get goin'. Nails is waitin'.

MATT (getting to his feet):
All right . . .

MAMIE (seizes his arm to pull him back):
Ain't you gonna kiss your baby?

She pulls him back far enough for him to kiss her. Tom, disgusted, gives them a razzberry.

TOM (mimicking Mamie):
Ain't you gonna kiss your baby? Nuts!

He turns away toward his own room.

139. BREAKFAST NOOK   CLOSE-UP
of Kitty seated at the table, sobbing softly.[23]

FADE OUT

FADE IN
140. STREET CORNER   BUSINESS SECTION   MEDIUM SHOT
Tom and Matt in their car waiting with the crowd of other vehicles for the signal. Crosstown traffic passing. Matt is driving, Tom seated beside him in the front seat. Just as the signal rings and Matt throws in his gears, Gwen steps from the crowd on the sidewalk on the curb and starts to cross. She is stunningly dressed and presents an attractive picture.

TOM (to Matt):
Hold on there, stupid! Slow down! There's a honey!

The car stops with a jerk. Gwen instinctively steps back. She looks Tom and Matt over coolly, then smiles slightly.

TOM:
How is it, babe?

GWEN:
Oh . . . I thought you were someone else.

TOM:
Oh, that's all right. Going south?

GWEN:
Yes . . . but I'm not in the habit of riding with strangers.

Tom jumps out of the car, opens the rear door.

TOM:
We don't need to be strangers.

Gwen hesitates, then steps into the car. Tom gets into the rear seat beside her.

TOM:
How far you going?

GWEN:
Pretty far, I'm afraid. Near Jackson Park. Is that out of your way?

TOM:
Oh no. My chauffeur is crazy about long drives.

He indicates Matt, who is turning to look at them and trying to keep in the party. He scowls at Tom. Tom assumes a haughty air and says,

TOM:
Step on it, Matt.

The car starts up.

141.   STREET

TRAVELING SHOT. Camera in front of the car picking up Matt at the wheel. Tom and Gwen in the back seat. Matt watching Gwen in the mirror, greatly interested. Tom also is all admiration. He looks Gwen over keenly without being able to think of anything to say.

GWEN:
    Well . . . do I look good to you?

TOM (embarrassed):
    You sure do.

GWEN:
    I feel flattered. You aren't the worst I've seen either.

TOM (after a moment's embarrassment):
    From Chicago?

GWEN:
    Not exactly. I came from Texas.

TOM:
    Where you living?

GWEN:
    Congress Hotel.[24]

MATT:
    If you're a stranger here, Tom and me will show you the town.

Tom glares at Matt with an expression that tells him to keep out of the conversation.

TOM:
    You drive your car.

Matt grins and turns back to the wheel.

                                          LAP DISSOLVE TO:

142.   STREET CORNER   RESIDENCE SECTION
The car drives in and stops.

GWEN:
> You can let me out here. I'm to meet some friends
> on the corner.

Tom gets out, opens the door, and Gwen steps out.

143.   STREET CORNER   CLOSE SHOT ON TOM AND GWEN
standing beside the car. Matt in driver's seat in the background.

TOM (after an awkward pause):
> Could . . . could I see you again . . . later?

GWEN:
> Why, I'd be delighted to have you call me some-
> time.

TOM:
> I mean, can't I see you later today?

GWEN (laughs):
> I'll think it over. Give me your phone number and
> I'll call you . . .

TOM (expansively):
> All right, babe. Yards 3771.

GWEN:
> Yards 3771. I'll remember it. Meanwhile, thanks
> very much. My name is Gwen . . . Gwen Allen.

TOM:
> Mine is Tom Powers.

MATT:
> And mine is . . .

TOM (interrupting with a scowl):
> He ain't got a name . . . just a number.

Gwen laughs and trips away with a little wave of her
hand. Both boys watch her in admiration, then Tom
jumps into the front seat and slams the door.

MATT:

> Gee! What a jane! I could go for her myself.

TOM:

> What do you mean you could go for her yourself?
> You'd go for an eighty-year-old chink with rheu-
> matism.

MATT:

> When you going to see her?

TOM:

> She's going to call me.

MATT:

> Find out if she's got a friend.

TOM:

> What do you want of a friend? You got Mamie, ain't
> you? (Mimicking.) Ain't you going to kiss your
> honey?

MATT:

> Well, you got Kittie, ain't you?

TOM:

> I ain't going to have her much longer. I'm getting
> fed up. And you can tell her so from me. Step on
> the gas.

The car drives out.

FADE OUT

FADE IN

144. INT. CAFE   FULL SHOT   NIGHT

One of the better-class cafes. The music is playing and
the dance floor is partially filled with couples. A rather
dressy crowd. The place is full, especially the tables
along the edge of the dance floor. There is a slight com-
motion among the waiters and the headwaiter. At the
entrance, someone of unusual importance. Headwaiter
hurries over toward door. Couple waiters follow.

145. INT. CAFE CLOSE SHOT AT DOOR

Nails with his girl Bess, a tall spectacular beauty; Paddy and Jane Daugherty; Tom and Gwen; Matt and Mamie, have just entered. Matt and Tom are wearing tuxedos for the first time. The whole party in dinner dress. Headwaiter hurries in with couple waiters at his elbow.

HEADWAITER (bowing profoundly):
Ah, Mr. Nathan. Delighted to see you, Mr. Nathan.

NAILS:
How are you, Joe?

JOE (HEADWAITER):
Fine, Mr. Nathan. Where will you sit?

NAILS (theatrically):
Where do I always sit? Right at the ringside.

PADDY:
It's all full up there.

HEADWAITER (quickly):
We can fix that, sir. (To waiters.) George . . . Eddie . . . fix a table for Mr. Nathan. Right there at the edge of the floor. (Pointing.)

NAILS:
Great! The best is none too good tonight! This is a wedding party, Joe![25] (Motioning toward Matt and Mamie.) Meet Mr. and Mrs. Doyle.

Matt and Mamie look sheepish and uncomfortable. The headwaiter bows profoundly.

HEADWAITER:
We're honored.

NAILS (to Bess):
Let's dance while they're fixing the table.

He gives his arm to Bess and they start toward dance floor. We TRUCK with them down the aisle toward the floor. Diners from all sides wave and bow, calling "Hello, Nails." Nails bestows bows and smiles to right and left as he walks along.

146.   INT. CAFE   CLOSE SHOT ON THE DANCE FLOOR
Nails and Bess appear on dance floor and dance off together. Paddy and Jane do the same. Tom and Gwen are just behind them. Gwen leads Tom awkwardly off onto the dance floor and they start in dancing.

147.   INT. CAFE   CLOSE SHOT ON TABLE
It is a table that has been set out on the edge of the floor. Waiters are arranging chairs for eight people. Matt and Mamie, who are the only ones not dancing, seat themselves at the table, look around the room as though for the first time that they have been there.

148.   INT. CAFE   CLOSE SHOT BY THE ORCHESTRA
The dance number finishes. Nails and Bess, who have been dancing in the foreground, stop. Nails goes over to master of ceremonies and whispers to him, pointing off at Matt and Mamie. Master of ceremonies looks in that direction, grins, and nods.

149.   INT. CAFE   CLOSE SHOT ON MATT AND MAMIE
alone at the table.

MAMIE (putting her hand over Matt's):
    Are you as happy as I am, Matt?

MATT (with an embarrassed grin):
    Sure.

MAMIE:
    You fellows don't realize what it means to a girl
    . . . getting married.

MATT (awkwardly):
    Well, you knew I was going to marry you all the
    time, didn't you?

MAMIE:
>   Sure. But I'm thinking of Tom and Kitty. (Her face shows a touch of sadness.)

MATT:
>   Aw, well . . . they're different. I guess Tom ain't the marryin' kind.

MAMIE (sadly):
>   No . . . I guess not.

They are interrupted by the return of Tom and Gwen, Paddy and Jane; last of all, Nails and Bess make their appearance, take their seats at the table. Nails leans over to whisper to Paddy and Jane. It is easy to see he is framing some sort of rib on Matt and Mamie.

150.   INT. CAFE   CLOSE SHOT ON MASTER OF CEREMONIES
He comes out in front of the orchestra wearing a very solemn expression. Holds up his hand for silence.

MASTER OF CEREMONIES:
>   Ladies and gentlemen, we are honored tonight by the presence of the very latest thing in bridal couples. We have with us, no other than Mr. *and Mrs.* Matthew Doyle.

He sweeps his hand toward Nails's table.

151.   INT. CAFE   MED. SHOT ON NAILS'S TABLE
All the diners at the nearby tables turn to look at Matt and Mamie with a cheer. Many of them raise glasses and call "To the bride," etc. Matt and Mamie greatly embarrassed.[26]

LAP DISSOLVE TO:

152.   DANCE FLOOR
Some time has passed. Floor is filled with dancers. In the foreground, Tom is dancing with Gwen. He stops suddenly and stares at someone he sees in a booth along the wall.

153.   INT. CAFE   CLOSE SHOT ON THE BOOTH
Putty Nose is just seating himself at the table opposite
from another man. He does not see Tom.

154.   INT. CAFE   CLOSE SHOT ON TOM AND GWEN
Tom stares at Putty Nose. Gwen looks around to see
what has attracted Tom's attention, but sees no one who
means anything to her. She takes Tom's arm and urges
him into the dance again.

LAP DISSOLVE TO:

155.   INT. CAFE   CLOSE SHOT ON NAILS'S TABLE
The girls are absent but Nails, Paddy, Tom, and Matt are
sitting there with drinks in front of them. Tom is silent
and sullen, Nails is ribbing him.

MATT (to Tom):
Are you sure it was old Putty Nose?

TOM:
I oughta know him, oughtn't I?

PADDY:
Sure you know him. (Jeering.) I suppose you want
to put in with him again?

NAILS (laughing):
That's the fagin that put something over on you,
ain't it? I had to laugh when I heard about it.

Nails looks intently at Tom who is silent and sullen, uncomfortable under his ribbing from Nails.

NAILS (sees he is getting a rise out of Tom):
That guy is going to take you again . . . probably
looking for you now. (Disdainfully.) He thinks
you're soft.

TOM (flaring up):
He's not going to take me!

MATT:
We don't want any part of him . . .

NAILS (waving his cigar in Tom's face):
    I ain't got a thing to say. He's got the Indian sign on
    you . . . and you're a cinch.

TOM (getting sore):
    In a pig's eye. That McGonagle ain't got a chance.

156.   INT. CAFE   CLOSE SHOT ON THE BOOTH
Putty Nose and his friend have finished their meal and
are just rising to leave. As he starts down the aisle
                                                    CUT TO:

157.   INT. CAFE   CLOSE SHOT ON NAILS'S TABLE
The party is all seated. Tom watching Putty Nose, turning his face to follow him down the room.

TOM (to Nails):
    Take care of the women, Nails.

NAILS (sarcastically):
    You're not going out into the dark, cold night?

TOM:
    C'mon, Matt. (To Gwen.) Nails'll see that you get
    home. We gotta job to do.

Gwen looks inquiringly from Tom to Nails. She senses
there is something in the air but can't quite get what it
is. Nails merely grins.

MAMIE (catching Matt's arm as he rises):
    You're not going to leave me tonight, Matt?

Matt hesitates, looks at Tom. Tom eyes him intently and
there is a command in his face.

MATT:
    There's something we forgot to do. I'll be home
    later.

TOM (gruffly):
    Come along!

He exits and Matt follows. Mamie watches, a little uncomfortable.

MAMIE:
Where are they going?

NAILS (laughs):
They're just going to walk around the block . . . until they cool off.

LAP DISSOLVE TO:

158.   EXT. GARAGE   NIGHT
Putty Nose comes out of the garage jauntily. Stops at the door and calls back to the attendant inside.

PUTTY NOSE:
Have her ready at eight o'clock . . . full of gas. I'm going on a long trip.

He starts jauntily down the street whistling to himself. TRUCK CAMERA with him. As he goes down the street a black cat suddenly runs across the sidewalk in front of him. He passes two or three houses, turns into the next one, taking the keys from his pocket. As he does so, Tom comes into the scene from across the street, Matt a few steps behind him.

159.   EXT. PUTTY'S HOUSE   CLOSE SHOT ON PUTTY NOSE
fitting the key into the lock. Tom and Matt come up behind him. He turns suddenly and sees them. Gives a start. Tom is cool, with a cool dead expression which gives Putty Nose a shiver.

PUTTY NOSE:
Well, if it ain't Tom Powers! And Matt too . . . how are you boys?

TOM:
Been out of town?

PUTTY NOSE (nervously):
Yeah . . . I was down home visitin'.

TOM:

> Gotta drink for us, Putty?

PUTTY:

> Sure, Tommy. But (nervously) I can't let you in. As usual I gotta jane in there. I'll bring it right out.

He opens the door and with a smirk starts in.

TOM (grasps his arm):

> No, you don't, Putty.

PUTTY (alarmed):

> What's up, Tom?[27] Drunk?

TOM:

> Never mind. We gotta little business to talk over . . . jane or no jane. (To Matt.) Come inside and close the door.

They disappear into the house. The door closes.

LAP DISSOLVE TO:

160.   PUTTY'S LIVING ROOM

Medium-sized room with ordinary furniture. Against one wall is an upright piano. Tom is standing facing Putty, who now is thoroughly alarmed.

PUTTY NOSE:

> What's wrong with you, Tom?

TOM:

> You know what's wrong. We ain't forgot how you lammed out on us after that fur hoist! Left us to take the rap!

Matt enters from an inside room.

MATT:

> A jane, huh? (To Tom.) There ain't nobody here except him.

TOM:

> I thought so.

He steps forward and hits Putty a blow on the jaw.

TOM:

> Sit down, you lyin', double-crossin' rat!

Putty sinks into a chair feeling of the bruise where Tom hit him with the pistol.

TOM:

> Don't make so much fuss over that bump! You gotta lot more comin'!

PUTTY NOSE (terrified):

> Gee, Tommy, Matt . . . what you gonna do? I don't wanna die!

TOM (scornfully):

> You don't wanna die? No?

PUTTY (pleading):

> Don't you remember, Tommy . . . and you, Matt . . . how you were just kids, and we were friends.

TOM:

> Nix on that soft stuff! You're going, and you know it!

MATT (who is holding aloof and letting Tom handle the matter):

> What are you going to do with him?

TOM:

> What does anyone do with a rat?[28]

PUTTY NOSE (in terror, throws his arms around Tom's legs, clutching him wildly):

> Don't let him, Matt! Don't let him! I'll do anything for you from now on! Ain't you gotta heart, Matty boy? I wouldn't hurt a fly! Remember how I used to play for you . . . tell me . . . don't you? Didn't I always stick up for you? I ain't got this comin' . . .

Tom looks at him coolly without replying—his deadly manner only terrifies Putty the more.

PUTTY NOSE:

>Please Matt . . . tell him not to! I ain't a bad fellow! *Oh, Tommy, Tommy, don't! Ain't you gotta heart?!* (Wildly to Matt.) You won't let him, Matt? You remember the old days! Remember that song I taught you . . .

He jumps over, runs to the piano, sits himself with his back to Tom and Matt, starts playing "Frankie and Johnnie."[29]

161.   PUTTY'S LIVING ROOM   CLOSE-UP OF MATT
He turns away as though the sight was a little bit too much for him. He is not going to take any more hand in it himself, but at the same time he's not going to interfere with Tom. We hear the piano off-scene, Putty playing, trying to sing the song in a cracked voice, quivering with terror. Matt watches him out of the corner of his eye. As he reaches the filthy lines where he was interrupted when playing in the clubroom, there is a sound of a pistol shot, then a crash of the keys as though someone had fallen forward with both arms on the keyboard. There is another shot. Matt turns away and walks toward the door, his face expressionless.

162.   CLOSE SHOT AT THE DOOR
Matt walks into the doorway from the living room, standing, waiting a moment. Tom appears from the living room, comes out past him, his face expressionless and his whole manner matter-of-fact.

TOM:

>Guess I'll ring up Gwen. She oughta be home by this time.

He starts out and Matt follows.[30]

FADE OUT

FADE IN
163.   GWEN'S APARTMENT   AFTERNOON
The sitting room of a high-class hotel suite. Gwen in a

stunning negligee is stretched out on a couch. Tom, ill at ease, is sitting in a chair. Between them is a little tab-oret of drinks laid out on it which they are sipping as they talk.

Tom is dressed much better and more fashionably than we have seen him before. Something is preying on his mind. His trouble is that Gwen is several notches higher in the social scale than any other girl he has known and he doesn't know how to handle her. Gwen realizes something of this and is playing with him in cat-and-mouse fashion.

GWEN:

> I may leave town next week, Tom. (Pause.) You don't care, do you?[31]

TOM (uncomfortable):

> Gee . . . if you go, you go . . . that's all.

GWEN (laughs and gets up):

> You're a funny boy. (She comes over to him, cups his face in her hands, and kisses him full on the lips.) You're a funny boy, but I like you immensely.

TOM:

> What's so funny about me?

GWEN:

> I don't mean funny in that sense. I mean you're different. (She goes back and sits on the couch, sips her drink.)

Tom is uncomfortable, silent for a moment, then starts to talk jerkily.

TOM:

> You know, when I met you I . . . well . . . I sort of figured you was on the make . . . not much . . . you know what I mean . . . then I sort of figured you was different too . . . that's from the girls' know. (Pause.) I never go for these long-winded

144

things. It's either yes or no. I couldn't figure you out.

GWEN (smiles):
And now can you?

TOM:
Naw. But I guess I'm not your kind . . . and we better call it quits.

GWEN:
Don't be that way, Tom. Of course I go for you, as you say . . . maybe too much.

TOM (darting a keen look at her):
You know all my friends think that . . . that things are different with us than they are.

GWEN:
Yes?

TOM:
Sure. They sort of think they know me . . . and they don't think I'd go for no merry-go-round.

GWEN:
Do you think I'm giving you a merry-go-round?

TOM:
No. I know . . .

GWEN:
Well then, do you want things to be different . . . to please your boyfriends?

TOM:
No . . . but . . . gee! How long can a guy hold out? (Jumps to his feet.) I'd go screwy! (He picks up his hat and starts for the door.)

GWEN:
Where are you going?

TOM:

> I'm gonna blow.

Tom stands silent, shifting his weight from one foot to the other. Gwen goes over, takes his hat from his hand, and throws it across the room.

GWEN:

> You're a spoiled boy, Tommy. You want things . . . and you aren't content until you get them. Well, maybe I'm spoiled too . . . maybe I feel that way too . . . But you're not running out on me like this. Come over here.

With mock indignation she leads him over to the couch, pushes him down onto it, and sits herself on his knees.

GWEN:

> Now you stay put, if you know what that means. (Puts her arms around him and draws his head down to her breast.) Oh, my bashful boy . . . (They are silent for a moment.) You are different, Tommy . . . very different. And I discovered that it's not only a difference in manner and outward appearances. It's a difference in basic character. Men that I know . . . and I've known dozens of them . . . they're so nice, so polished, so considerate. Most women like that type. I guess they're afraid of any other kind. I thought I was too . . . but you're so *strong!* You don't give . . . you take! Oh, Tommy! I could love you to death!

She takes his face in her hands and covers it with kisses. Tom suddenly seizes her violently in his arms and returns the caress. Doorbell rings off-scene. Both Tom and Gwen give a start.

TOM (disgusted at the interruption):

> Aw, nuts!

Gwen gets up and walks toward the door. Tom also gets up and strolls about the room with his hands in his pockets.

164.   INT. GWEN'S APARTMENT   CLOSE SHOT AT THE DOOR
Gwen opens the door. Matt, wild-eyed and excited, bursts in.

MATT:
　　Tom here? (He sees Tom.) Tom . . . Nails . . .

Tom walks into the scene. He is angry at Matt for the interruption. He glowers at him.

MATT (excitedly):
　　Nails . . . dead . . .

Tom stands stupefied for a moment. Then steps forward and grabs Matt fiercely by the arm.

TOM (furiously):
　　What's that?

Matt, out of breath, can only nod vigorously. Tom relaxes his hold, stands stupefied for a moment, then fury rises to his face.

TOM:
　　Who did it?

MATT:
　　Nobody . . . his horse! Threw him off in the park . . . kicked him in the head!

Tom is too stunned to reply. He looks around helplessly for a moment, sinks into a chair. Gwen comes over, pats his shoulder sympathetically. Tom suddenly gets to his feet, jams his hat on his head, and without a word to Gwen strides out of the apartment. Matt follows.

FADE OUT

FADE IN
165.   LIVERY STABLE　　　　　　　　　　　　　　　　DAY
　　A SHOT just inside the door. The usual equipment of a

stable where high-grade riding horses are kept. Bridles, saddles, etc., hanging on the walls. Sitting just inside the door is an attendant reading the newspaper. Tom and Matt walk in. They are dressed immaculately in the clothes they have worn to the funeral—black frock coats, pin-striped trousers, flowers in their lapels, gloves, etc. They wear very solemn, intent expressions. Very crisp and businesslike.

TOM:
You got that horse that killed Nails Nathan?

ATTENDANT:
You mean, Rajah? (Shakes his head sadly.) A bad animal. Terrible . . . terrible!

MATT:
What's he worth?

ATTENDANT:
Very spirited horse. I told Mr. Nathan not to ride him.

TOM (fiercely):
What's he worth?

ATTENDANT:
Well . . . he could be bought for a thousand dollars. You see he's . . .

TOM:
Never mind. (Takes a roll of bills out of his pocket.) Here. (Sticks a thousand dollars into the attendant's hand.)

MATT:
Where's he at?

ATTENDANT (pointing off):
Stall number four.

Tom and Matt start off in the direction that the attendant indicates. Attendant follows.

TOM (turning to the attendant):
    Stay where you are.

Attendant stops, surprised and alarmed. He watches as Tom and Matt disappear toward the stall. Doesn't know what to make of this. His face shows growing amazement at what he sees off-scene. Hold him this way for a moment, then we hear a shot fired off-scene, followed by a heavy fall. The attendant gives a gasp of amazement. In a moment, Tom and Matt reenter. Tom is carrying a horse's blanket with the name Rajah on it. He throws it at the attendant's feet.

TOM:
    Maybe you can use it. (Motioning with his head toward the stall.) It's a cinch he never will.[32]

Tom and Matt stride toward the door, leaving the attendant watching them, open mouthed. At the door they turn.

166.   LIVERY STABLE   CLOSE-UP OF TOM AND MATT
turning to look back at the attendant, tears showing in their eyes.

TOM (with a gulp in his voice):
    That's the last man he'll ever murder.

                               FADE OUT

FADE IN

167.   INT. POWERS KITCHEN   DAY
Mrs. Powers at the stove stirring something in a pot. She is in a housedress with an apron over it. Tom is standing behind the kitchen table in a new tailored suit, looking very swagger.

MRS. POWERS (solicitous):
    Aw, Tommy, let me make you a cup of tea.

TOM:
    I've got to be getting on the job, Ma.

MRS. POWERS (leaves her cooking and comes over and puts her arms around him):
> My, but it's good to see you. I was beginning to think I'd lost you.

TOM (amused):
> You can't lose me so easy.

MRS. POWERS (shaking her head sadly):
> Poor Michael. I'm afraid he's working himself into an early grave. Days on the cars . . . school at night, and studying in between.

TOM (nods):
> Well, listen, Ma, I come over to give you somethin'. (Pulls roll of bills out of his pocket.) Take this . . . and when you need more, just say so. I'm making plenty.

Mrs. Powers looks at the money and gasps at the size of the roll.

168. POWERS LIVING ROOM   CLOSE SHOT AT THE FOOT OF THE STAIRS
Mike is coming down the stairs with his conductor's cap on, his uniform coat over his arm. Stops at the bottom of the stairs and starts to put on his coat.

169. POWERS KITCHEN
Mrs. Powers is holding the roll of bills, undecided just what to do with them.

MRS. POWERS:
> Tommy, you're a good boy, but . . . I can't . . . Michael won't like it. He . . .

TOM:
> Mike ain't got anything to say about it.

MIKE (off-scene):
> No?

He advances into the scene, then stands in front of Tom who turns to look at him with the beginning of a sneer. Mrs. Powers lays the roll of bills on the table as though afraid to be caught with them.

MIKE:
Listen to me, Tom, I've got something to say . . . and it's important.

TOM:
Keep it to yourself. No one's asking you to stick your nose in.

MRS. POWERS:
I don't want you boys fighting . . . it ain't right . . . for two brothers . . .

TOM:
There ain't going to be no fight to this, Ma . . . but I don't need his preaching.

MIKE (points to the money on the table):
What's this, Ma?

MRS. POWERS (timidly):
Tommy just gave it to me to . . . to buy some things. (Nervously.) Ain't that nice of him?

TOM:
Don't you like it? It's more than you can do.

MIKE:
We don't want your money. I'm taking care of Ma.

TOM (sneering):
On two bits a week.

MIKE:
Ma doesn't go to nightclubs and she doesn't drink champagne.

MRS. POWERS (making a timid attempt to humor him):
Now, Michael, how do you know? I used to dance when I was a girl.

MIKE:

> Listen, Tom . . . I ain't going to argue with you, and I can't say all I want to in front of Ma . . . but get an earful of this! You ain't welcome in this house!

MRS. POWERS (moves in between the boys):
> Michael!

MIKE (pushing her slightly aside):
> That money is blood money! We want no part of it! (Picks up money and holds it out to Tom, who ignores it.)

TOM:
> Hiding behind Ma's skirt . . . like always . . .

MIKE:
> Better than hiding behind machine guns!

TOM:
> You're too smart. (To Mrs. Powers.) I'm going, Ma.

MIKE (holding out the money):
> And don't forget your change.

TOM:
> Money don't mean nothin' to me.

MIKE (contemptuously):
> I guess not. But with no heart and no brains, it's all you got. You'll need it.

Tom with fire in his eyes grabs Mike by the lapels of his coat. He holds the two lapels together with his left hand and draws back his right with doubled fist.

TOM:
> You stoolin', sneakin' . . . I'll beat . . .

Mike breaks loose from Tom and slams him on the jaw.

MRS. POWERS (frantically trying to separate them):
> Tommy! Michael!

Mike allows Mrs. Powers to part them. He steps back but he still glares at Tom who returns the glare with insolence. Then Mike stuffs the money violently into Tom's hand. Tom savagely tears the money in half, throws the pieces into Mike's face, turns on his heel, and exits.

MRS. POWERS (brokenly; on the verge of tears):
Tommy! Don't go . . . that way again . . . please.

Mike turns and puts his arm around Mrs. Powers, pats her on the shoulder consolingly.

FADE OUT

FADE IN
170. EXT. PADDY'S SALOON   DAY
The whole front of the place has been wrecked by a bomb. Sidewalk is covered with debris. A crowd gathered and policemen keeping them moving. Fire apparatus in the street, just standing by, although there is no sign of fire.

VOICE (from the crowd):
What was it? A bomb?

ANOTHER VOICE:
Must have been ten bombs! Heard it clear up at my place.[33]

171. INT. PADDY'S BACK ROOM
The place shows the effect of the bombing. Plaster on the floor, couple of chairs broken, tables disarranged, etc. Paddy is standing by one of the tables in a fierce argument with Tom, Matt, Dutch, and Bugs. All of them are excited and Tom is particularly ferocious.

TOM:
. . . nobody's going to get away with anything like that! I know who they are . . . and where to find them!

153

PADDY:

Now lie down! This is my turn to talk!

TOM:

But I'm tellin' you . . .

PADDY:

I'm tellin' *you!* (Turns to the others.) All of you! You guys are in a hot seat and don't know it! You're going to lay low for a few days! I've got a gaff out south where you can hide out till I can get the mob together again!

TOM:

I ain't going to hide out!

PADDY:

No? You're just going to walk out and take it in the head, I suppose?

MATT:

Who's going to do it?

PADDY:

Who ain't? Right now we ain't got a chance! Since Nails is gone his mob has scattered! They're ten to one against us! Look at this! (Indicating the wreckage and ruin.) Four pineapples tossed at us in two days . . . and the brewery set afire. I'm tellin' you they got us on the run!

TOM:

I ain't runnin' . . . I ain't yellow . . .

PADDY:

Who said you was? I ain't talking about that. I'm going to need you . . . and you won't be any good to me when you're in a cemetery! I've got to have a few days to get the boys lined up again. And while I'm doing that you're going to be where nobody knows where to find you, except me! Have I ever steered you wrong? Have I?

MATT:

> No. (To Tom.) He's right, Tom.

Tom nods.

PADDY:

> That's more like it. Now listen . . . as soon as it gets
> dark, Joe Penny'll come up the alley with a closed
> car . . .

FADE OUT

FADE IN

172. JANE DAUGHERTY'S DINING ROOM

A well-furnished dining room on the ground floor of a
private house. Through the archway we get the glimpse
of the living room beyond. This latter room has windows on the street front of the building. Paddy, Tom,
Matt, Dutch, and Bugs are at the dining room table.
Jane, in an attractive housedress, is at a buffet in the
background getting out some drinks. Dutch and Bugs
are running their eyes around the room as though examining the place. Tom and Matt are sullen and resent-
ful at their imprisonment.

PADDY:

> Now give me your guns and your money . . . all of
> it!

TOM:

> What are ya trying to pull, Paddy?

PADDY:

> I'm going to keep you off the streets. Even *you* ain't
> sap enough to go for a stroll without your gat!
> C'mon! Shower down!

The boys, grumbling, start taking their guns out of their
belts. They lay them on the table, reach in their pockets
for their money. As they're doing this Jane places a tray
with glasses and a bottle on one end of the table.

TOM (as he brings out his money):
> Got a phone here, Jane? I'm going to ring up Gwen.[34]

PADDY (sternly):
> No! Keep away from the phone! I'll call up from outside and tell her I had to send you out of town for a few days.

MATT (as he shells out his money):
> And ring up Mamie, also.

PADDY:
> Leave it to me. (He collects the guns and money.) This won't be for long, boys. I'll have the mob lined up again in a couple of days. Jane, you'll see that they're comfortable.

JANE (smiling as she pulls cork from bottle):
> You can leave that to *me*, Paddy.

PADDY:
> Okay.

He starts out with the guns and the money. Jane pours a drink.

JANE (gaily):
> Gather around, boys. We're going to be a happy little family.

TOM:
> I hope you got plenty of that medicine.

He takes a glass. The other boys gather around and help themselves to the drinks as Jane pours them.

173.   ALLEY   CLOSE SHOT ON A GARAGE
which opens directly on the alley. Paddy sticks his head out of the garage door and surveys the alley in both directions cautiously, then disappears.

174.   ALLEY   CLOSE SHOT ON HACK MILLER
hiding behind an outbuilding a few yards down from
the garage, peeking out. He registers that he has seen
Paddy.

175.   ALLEY   CLOSE SHOT ON THE GARAGE
Paddy drives his car out of the garage and turns down
the alley.

176.   ALLEY   CLOSE SHOT ON HACK MILLER
in his hiding place. He watches cautiously until Paddy
has driven away, then sneaks out and steals down the
alley.

                                          LAP DISSOLVE TO:

177.   CLOSE-UP OF HACK
dropping a coin in the slot of a public telephone.[35]

                                          FADE OUT

FADE IN

178.   JANE'S LIVING ROOM   NIGHT
Tom is seated in an armchair in the foreground, an
empty glass in his hand. He is more than half drunk.
Jane is sitting beside him. They have evidently been
having a conversation and Jane is plainly attracted to
him. Through the archway we see Matt, Bugs, and
Dutch playing cards on the dining room table. The curtains in both rooms are drawn. Tom is nodding and apparently going to sleep on Jane.

JANE:
Let me fix you another drink, Tommy?

TOM (thickly):
Gee . . . mean to say you've got any of the stuff
left?

JANE (laughs):
Oh, you haven't drank so much. (She takes the
glass and starts out.)

TOM:
> Well . . . I can drink it as long as you can pour it.
> (His head nods again.)

Just as Jane reaches the dining room arch, there is a sharp staccato rattle heard from outside. Tom jumps to his feet, awake instantly. The boys at the table jump up, stand a moment listening, then come stealthily into the living room, all of them alarmed. Tom raises his hand as a signal to keep silent, then tiptoes over to the front window, cautiously pulls the shade aside, and peeks out.

179.   STREET
In front of Jane's house. A coal truck is backing up to the curb and coal is pouring down the metal chute making the rattle which the boys heard. The driver stands beside the truck. His eyes are fixed on an upper window across the street. The truck is between him and Jane's house so that Tom can't see him.

180.   JANE'S LIVING ROOM   CLOSE SHOT ON TOM
peeking out the window. The other boys just behind him. Jane edges in and stands listening tensely. Tom turns back, drops the shade with a grin of relief.

TOM:
> Just a coal truck. Had me going for a minute though.

The other boys take deep breaths of relief and exit toward the dining room.

MATT (turning back for a moment):
> Come and get in the game, Tom.

TOM:
> Naw . . . I'm going to hit the hay.

JANE:
> I'll show you your room.

She leads the way out and Tom follows.

181.   STREET   CLOSE SHOT ON THE COAL TRUCK
The driver standing beside it makes a careful guarded signal toward the upper part of the house across the street, nods as though getting a reply, and shuts off the coal.

182.   FURNISHED ROOM
This is a small front room on the upper floor of the house across the street from Jane's. The room itself is in darkness. We shoot from the rear of the room toward the window and get in silhouette the figures of two hoodlums standing guard over two machine guns mounted on tripods and trained on the entrance of Jane's house. Through the window we see Jane's house and the coal truck across the street. The machine gunners are silent and watchful. Both of them are smoking. One of them lights a cigarette from the butt of one he is smoking and drops the butt on the floor.

183.   JANE'S BEDROOM
A small bedroom with a single bed and reading lamp. Light from the reading lamp on the table. Tom is standing up by the bed unsteadily. He has taken off his coat and has started to unbutton his shirt. He is so drunk that he is clumsy. Has difficulty with his button. Jane enters with a drink in her hand.

JANE:
I thought you might like a nightcap, Tommy?

Tommy instinctively reaches for his coat to cover himself up. Jane laughs.

JANE:
You don't need to be ashamed with me, Tommy. Here, let me help you.

She places the drink on the table, closes the door gently. Comes over and begins unbuttoning Tom's shirt.

TOM (embarrassed):
> Naw. I don't need no help.

He tries to push Jane away, but she laughingly insists on helping him.

JANE:
> Keep still now and be a good boy. Sit down.

Pushes him down on the bed. Tom is too dizzy from his drinks to protest any further.

JANE:
> I'll take your shoes and socks off, too. I feel like I'm undressing my child.

Tom says nothing. His head drops helplessly. Jane gets his shirt off, then she suddenly straightens up and puts her arm around his neck.

JANE:
> You don't think I'm old, do you, Tom?

Tom closes his eyes and shakes his head wearily.

JANE:
> I'm still young, am I not?[36]

TOM (sleepily):
> Sure.

Jane bends down suddenly, brings her mouth to his, holding him in a tight embrace.

TOM (struggling to free himself):
> Here . . . what's the big idea?

JANE (removes her mouth from his):
> Just a good night kiss for a fine boy.

She straightens up, runs her hand through Tom's hair. Tom makes no protest. Jane suddenly leans over toward the table and switches off the light.

FADE OUT

FADE IN

184. FURNISHED ROOM CLOSE-UP DAY

of a pile of cigarette butts between the feet of the two machine gunners. Another butt still smoking is dropped onto the pile. There are several dozen of the butts indicating that the men have been watching and smoking all night.

185. JANE'S DINING ROOM

Jane is arranging breakfast on the table. Tom enters fully dressed but showing the effects of a hangover.

JANE (brightly):
  Breakfast's all ready, Tommy.

TOM (surly):
  I ain't hungry.

Jane glances out in the next room to see that no one else is in sight, comes up close to Tom.

JANE (coyly):
  You aren't sorry, are you?

TOM:
  Sorry? For what?

JANE:
  For . . . for last night.

TOM:
  What do you mean . . . getting drunk?

JANE:
  Aren't you the little play actor?

She pats his hand fondly. Tom begins to get some idea of what she is talking about. He is amazed, then furious.

TOM:
  Wait a minute! Do you mean . . . ?

Jane with a smile playfully puts her hand across his mouth, coyly pantomiming for him to keep still. Tom now throughly aroused knocks her hand away.

TOM:
> You . . . you . . .

Then in a sudden burst of anger he gives Jane a resounding slap on the face, turns away, and strides out of the room leaving Jane watching him in blank dismay.

186.   JANE'S LIVING ROOM
Tom strides through. His face furious. He picks up his hat from the table and jams it on his head and he strides on through the front door just as Matt enters.

MATT:
> Tom . . . where you going?

TOM:
> Home.

MATT:
> But Paddy said . . .

TOM:
> I don't care what Paddy said! I'm getting out of this dump!

He strides on out toward the front door. Matt stands undecided for a second, then grabs his own hat from the table and starts after him.[37]

187.   STREET   CLOSE SHOT ON THE COAL TRUCK
It has evidently been standing there all night. The driver, peering around the truck toward Jane's house, sees Tom and Matt. He gives a signal across the street, opens the trap, and the coal begins to rattle down the chute.

188.   FURNISHED ROOM   CLOSE SHOT ON THE MACHINE
       GUNNERS
       Noise of the coal heard off-scene. The gunners get the
signals from across the street, see Tom and Matt, and
immediately go into action, the noise of the machine
guns mingling with the clatter of the coal. Hold on them
for a few moments.

189.   EXT. JANE'S HOUSE
       A SHOT at the side where there is a passage between it
and the next house. The machine guns and coal heard
off-scene. Tom comes dashing around the corner into
the shelter of the house. As he does so a couple of bullets tear splinters off the corner of the house. Tom stops,
creeps carefully back toward the corner, peeks out. As
he does so, another splinter is torn off by a bullet and
Tom ducks back. He stands for a moment, his face
working with dismay and fury. Then with an expression
which shows there is nothing he can do about it, he
turns and runs down the passage.

190.   STREET
       Flash of crowds running past, dashing out of houses,
two or three uniformed policemen coming on the run.

191.   EXT. JANE DAUGHERTY'S HOUSE
       CLOSE SHOT by the front sidewalk. Matt is lying on the
sidewalk crumpled up in a heap, dead, blood trickling
in a stream across the sidewalk.

                                          FADE OUT

FADE IN
192.   GWEN'S APARTMENT   DAY
       It is the same room in which we saw Tom and Gwen
before. The room is empty but immediately we hear the
rattling of the key in the lock. Door is opened and Tom
enters, closing the door quickly behind him. He has the

air of a hunted man. He takes a deep breath of relief once he is safe inside the apartment.

TOM (calling):
Gwen! (Walks over to the bedroom door, looks in.) Where are you, babe?

Turns back as he sees Gwen is not there. Disappointed. Goes over to the window, looks out cautiously down the street to make sure no one has followed him. Goes over to the wall phone, takes down the receiver.

TOM (in phone):
Yards 1771. (Waits a moment.)

193.   INT. PADDY'S SALOON   CLOSE-UP OF ERNIE AT THE TELEPHONE

ERNIE (at phone):
Who is it? Not Tom? No, Paddy's not here. Yeah . . . he's down to the district attorney's office. Yeah . . . They got him on the carpet. Sure. Some of Schemer Burns's work.

194.   INT. GWEN'S APARTMENT   CLOSE SHOT ON TOM AT THE PHONE

He hangs up, turns away. Here is more bad luck. Walks over toward a cabinet against the wall. PAN with him as he goes to cabinet. He opens it, takes out a whiskey bottle and glass. Then he notices for the first time a note lying on top of the cabinet. He puts down the bottle and picks up the note. Reads it. His face goes blank. He stares at the note, lays it down on the cabinet, his face a picture of dismay. Rage growing within him. He gets a corkscrew from the cabinet, starts to pull the cork from the bottle. It is too slow a process for him and with a snarl of rage he grabs the bottle, smashes the end of it against the cabinet, and knocks off the neck. Pours out a stiff drink. Picks up the note again and reads it a second time.

WE INSERT CLOSE-UP OF THE LAST LINES OF A NOTE IN GWEN'S HANDWRITING:

> . . . and so the best thing for me to do
> is go back home. Always remember me,
> Tommy, as one who loved you with all
> the love at her command.
>
> Gwen

BACK TO SCENE:

Tom looks up from the note in a rage. Everything has slipped out from under him. With a snarl, he tears the note in two and throws it aside. Gulps his drink, pours another, turns away, and stands in deep thought, his rage growing rapidly until it reaches the point of ferocity. He comes to a decision which shows in his face as a terrible menace. He quickly rummages in the drawers of the cabinet looking for a gun. He doesn't find one but finds a handful of bullets.

CLOSE-UP OF TOM'S HAND FILLED WITH LARGE-CALIBER BULLETS

BACK TO SCENE:

Tom stuffs the bullets in his coat pocket, jams his hat down on his head, and strides toward the door.[38]

LAP DISSOLVE TO:

195. INT. PAWNSHOP

Pawnbroker behind the counter near the window, which is filled with the usual odds and ends found in pawnbroker's display. Pawnbroker arranging some of the articles as Tom enters. Tom is pretending to be diffident and awkward so as not to arouse the pawnbroker's suspicions.

PAWNBROKER (briskly):
    Yes, sir?

TOM (diffidently):
    I was lookin' at them pistol things in the window.

PAWNBROKER (all business):
Let me show you some.

TOM:
I kinda like that big one (pointing) there.

Pawnbroker brings out a .45-caliber revolver, hands it to Tom, who takes it as though it was something strange.

TOM:
What do you call this?

PAWNBROKER:
That's a .45-caliber Smith & Wesson. It's a fine . . . [39]

TOM:
Got any more?

PAWNBROKER:
I have some smaller ones.

TOM:
No . . . the same size.

Pawnbroker brings out a second pistol like the first.

TOM:
How do you load it?

PAWNBROKER (taking the pistol):
You break it. (Breaking pistol.) Slip the cartridges into these holes. (Pointing.)

TOM:
Could I see?

He takes pistol which is still broken, reaches in his pocket, gets several cartridges, slips them into chamber. Quickly closes the pistol then points it at the pawnbroker.

TOM (suddenly stern and menacing):
Stick 'em up!

Pawnbroker gives a sickly grin, thinking it is a joke, but as he looks into Tom's eyes he sees Tom means business. The grin fades and the pawnbroker's hands go into the air. Tom keeps him covered, picks up the other pistol off the case, backs out of the room, keeping the terrified pawnbroker covered with the gun.

FADE OUT

FADE IN

196. STREET RAIN CLOSE SHOT OF TOM   NIGHT
standing in the shelter of the buildings, keeping an intent watch on something across the street. He is drunk, ferocious. It is plain from his mood that he will allow nothing to interfere with his plan. The noise of two automobiles heard off-scene. Tom's gaze becomes suddenly more intent. A menacing leer spreads across his face as he recognizes the people he has been waiting for.

197. EXT. BURNS HEADQUARTERS
A large dingy building in the middle of the block. Sign over the door Western Chemical Company. There is a door leading to a stairway and a store front with plate glass windows in the front of the building. Two cars drive up and stop and Schemer Burns and six or eight of his hoodlums, including Hack Miller and the two machine gunners who killed Matt, get out of them. They are laughing and chatting together. They exit into the stairway door.

198. STREET CLOSE SHOT ON TOM
He waits until all the men are inside the building, then thrusts his hands in his pockets and strides slowly and deliberately across the street. TRUCK CAMERA just ahead of him to hold him all the way across. A look of deadly menace on his face.

199.   EXT. BURNS HEADQUARTERS
Tom enters in the same deadly manner and, without
pausing or breaking his stride, exits into the building.
Hold on the doorway for a few seconds, then suddenly
an uproar of shots, yells, and curses breaks out from
inside. In a moment Tom runs out, whirls around, and
fires a last shot into the doorway. He pulls the trigger
again but his gun is empty. He takes it by the barrel and
hurls it ferociously through the plate glass windows of
the storefront. He hurls the other gun through the other
window, turns, and runs for his car. As he runs out of
the scene one of the hoodlums dashes out of the doorway and fires rapidly at Tom. Then the hoodlum staggers, grasps his side with a grimace of pain, and crum-
ples up in the gutter.[40]

200.   STREET
FLASH of pedestrians who have heard the shots coming
on a run from all directions.

201.   STREET CORNER
Flash of a uniformed policeman. He blows his whistle
and starts on a run down the street.

202.   STREET   CLOSE SHOT ON TOM
staggering across the street. He has evidently been hit
several times, clutches at a wounded arm, sinks to his
knees, tries to crawl the rest of the way. He is badly
wounded but still alive. A policeman and one or two
pedestrians run in and surround him excitedly.

                                        FADE OUT

        FADE IN
203.   HOSPITAL CORRIDOR   CLOSE SHOT   DAY
just outside the door to a private room. A uniformed
policeman is on guard sitting in a chair just outside the
door. The door opens and Paddy and the hospital doctor come out of the room. Both very solemn.

DOCTOR:
Can't say.

PADDY:
Well, we can hope for the best . . .

Paddy gives the doctor a signal for silence as Mrs. Powers, Mike, and Molly come down the corridor.

PADDY (to doctor):
This is Tom's mother and brother, Doctor.

DOCTOR (bowing):
You can go in for a few minutes, Mrs. Powers.

He stands aside as Mrs. Powers and Molly enter the room. Mike hangs back but gives a questioning look at Paddy. Paddy shakes his head slightly to indicate the case is very serious. Mike nods slightly, turns into the room.

204.   HOSPITAL ROOM   CLOSE SHOT ON BED
Tom is lying in bed, his face swathed in bandages, his eyes covered. One arm lying outside the bedspread. A nurse hovering around the bed, doing everything to make him comfortable. Mrs. Powers followed by Molly and Mike come up to the bed. She looks at Tom almost in awe for a moment. Then leans over.

MRS. POWERS (gently):
Tommy . . . Tommy boy. Do you know me?

Tom nods very feebly, lifts his hand weakly, groping in the dark. Mrs. Powers takes his hand in both of hers.

MRS. POWERS:
Mike's here, Tommy. He came to see you.

TOM (feebly):
Hello . . . Mike . . .

MIKE (coming over to the bed):
How are you Tom, old scout?

Tom releases his hand from his mother's grasp and
gropes again to get Mike's. Mike takes his hand in a
warm clasp.

205. CLOSE-UP OF THE TWO HANDS CLASPING

TOM (voice off-scene):
>   Been . . . been . . . wanting to . . . see you,
>   Mike . . .

MIKE (voice off-scene):
>   You're going to be seeing a lot of me.

206. HOSPITAL ROOM   CLOSE-UP OF MRS. POWERS
her eyes full of tears but her face radiant as she watches
the two boys.

207. HOSPITAL ROOM   CLOSE SHOT ON TOM AND MIKE
Tom has released the grasp of Mike's hand and his own
hand is lying on the covers.

TOM (feebly):
>   I . . . I had something to . . . to tell you. I . . . I'm
>   sorry . . .

MIKE:
>   Sorry for what?

TOM:
>   Just . . . sorry . . . you know.

208. HOSPITAL ROOM   CLOSE-UP OF MRS. POWERS
her eyes full of tears but her face radiant.

MRS. POWERS:
>   Oh, Tommy! You and Mike are going to be friends
>   again?

TOM (off-scene):
>   Sure . . . friends.

MRS. POWERS:
> Oh, boys! How happy . . . how happy . . .

She breaks down. Her face covered with tears. Takes out a handkerchief to wipe her eyes.

209. HOSPITAL ROOM   CLOSE SHOT ON THE GROUP
Mrs. Powers weeping. Molly, also greatly affected, puts her arm around her.

TOM (weakly):
> I . . . I've been . . . thinking things. I . . . I was the sucker . . . not Mike. Ma . . . you must like Mike . . . a lot better than me . . .

MRS. POWERS:
> No, no, Tommy! You're my baby!

TOM:
> Sure. I . . . I'm your baby . . . Ma.

MRS. POWERS:
> Oh, Tommy, you're coming home, ain't you? To stay?

TOM:
> Sure . . . coming home. It . . . it ain't no use . . . Nails . . . Matt . . . gone . . . sure, coming home.[41] If I . . . ever get out . . .

MIKE:
> You're going to get out all right, Tom.

MRS. POWERS (seizing Tom's hand):
> Of course you are, Tommy boy. You're going to get well and strong. (She kisses his hand.) Both of my boys back . . . all of us together again. I'm . . . I'm almost glad this happened.

Mike turns away greatly affected as Mrs. Powers is talking. He exchanges a look with Molly. It is evident they don't share Mrs. Powers's confidence in Tom's recovery.
> FADE OUT

FADE IN

210.　POWERS LIVING ROOM　　　　　　　　　　　NIGHT

Mike is sitting in the living room at the table studying a book. Through the dining room door we get a glimpse of Mrs. Powers and Molly bustling around the table, getting dinner ready. Mrs. Powers humming a snatch of some well-known Irish song. She is very happy. She comes to the dining room door and stops.

MRS. POWERS:
　　He really looked better today? Did he, Michael?

MIKE (looking up from his book):
　　Sure, Ma. A lot better. He was sitting up. I told him you'd be back again tomorrow.[42]

Mrs. Powers smiles happily. Goes back into the dining room resuming her humming. Mike resumes his studying for a moment. There is a gentle rap at the door. Mike listens; the rap is repeated. He gets up and goes to the door.

211.　POWERS LIVING ROOM　　CLOSE SHOT AT THE DOOR

Mike enters and opens the door revealing Paddy standing just outside, with a very serious look on his face.

MIKE:
　　Oh, Paddy, come in.

Paddy signals for Mike to come out. He is very serious. Mike, mystified, steps out onto the porch.

212.　POWERS PORCH

lighted by the lights from the living room window. Mike comes out and Paddy signals for him to close the door. He closes it gently.

MIKE:
　　What's wrong? Is Tom . . .

172

PADDY:

They kidnapped him from the hospital this afternoon.

MIKE (astounded):

What? Who did?

PADDY (signaling for Tom to speak lower):

Must have been the Burns mob. First they gave it to him in the back . . . then they take him when he's helpless! Who knows what they're doing to him now!

MIKE:

They ain't going to get away with this!

PADDY:

I'm doing all I can. All the boys are out on the streets! I'm going to get Tom back, if it's the last thing I do!

MIKE:

I'm gonna . . .

PADDY:

You're gonna stay here . . . right by the phone, and wait for messages. I told the boys to call you up when they find anything . . .

MIKE (bitterly):

I'd like to smash . . .

PADDY (interrupting):

I've sent word to Burns that if he'll send Tom home, tonight, I'll quit the racket! They can have it all! I'll leave town and never come back!

MIKE:

Do you think they'll do it?

PADDY:

It's a sweet offer . . . you just stay here. And if you

hear of anything from my boys, call me at my place. I gotta get on the job now.

He hurries away leaving Mike staring blankly out into the street.

LAP DISSOLVE TO:

213. POWERS DINING ROOM

Mrs. Powers, Molly, and Mike at dinner. Mike wears a very serious brooding expression. Molly notices this but says nothing.

MRS. POWERS:
> What's the matter, Michael? Don't you like your dinner?

MIKE:
> I . . . I just ain't very hungry, Ma.

There is silence again for a few moments, then the phone in the living room rings. Mrs. Powers starts to get up but Michael jumps to his feet immediately.

MIKE:
> I'll get it.

He hurries off to the living room. Mrs. Powers, uneasy, follows him.

214. POWERS LIVING ROOM   CLOSE SHOT ON MIKE AT THE PHONE

MIKE (in phone):
> Yeah. This is Mike. (Suddenly excited.) When? You are? Fine.

He hangs up the receiver, turns around excitedly as Mrs. Powers enters, looks at him questioningly.

MIKE (eagerly):
> Ma, they're bringing Tom home.

MRS. POWERS:
They are? When?

MIKE:
Right now. He's on the way.

MRS. POWERS:
Is he . . . is he all right?

MIKE (confident):
He must be, or they wouldn't bring him home.

MRS. POWERS (happily excited):
Oh, it's wonderful! I'll get his room ready. I knew
my baby would come home.

She hurries out as Molly comes to the dining room door.

MOLLY:
Who called, Mike?

MIKE:
One of Paddy's boys . . . I guess. Didn't say who.

MRS. POWERS (voice off-scene):
Molly . . . Molly dear.

MOLLY:
Yes, Mother.

MRS. POWERS (off-scene):
Bring up some clean sheets from the linen closet.
Hurry!

MOLLY:
All right.

She exits. Mike paces the floor excited but greatly relieved.

215.   POWERS BEDROOM
The same room that Tom and Mike occupied as boys.
Mrs. Powers is bustling about happily and excited,

making the bed. She is singing the Irish song in a louder voice than before.

216.   POWERS LIVING ROOM
Mike still pacing the floor waiting. There is a sudden rap at the door. It comes as Mike is at the far end of the room. He turns immediately and hurries toward the door. Before he reaches it, we hear the sound of an automobile starting up, growing fainter as it drives away.

217.   POWERS LIVING ROOM   CLOSE SHOT AT THE DOOR
Mike strides in. Opens the door. As he does so the dead body of Tom, which has been propped against the door, falls into the room. Mike jumps aside in amazement. Body falls on the floor face down and Mike stares at it, slowly kneels, turns it over, gasps in horror, then turns body back on its face. Slowly gets up, his expression one of dismay and horror.

218.   POWERS LIVING ROOM   CLOSE-UP OF MIKE
staring down at Tom in horror.

219.   POWERS BEDROOM
Mrs. Powers bustling about the bed, smoothing down the sheets, singing her Irish song happily.

220.   POWERS LIVING ROOM   CLOSE SHOT
on Mike standing by Tom's body. The horror on his face gradually giving way to a look of fury. He comes to a decision, turns, and strides toward the closet.[43]

221.   CLOSET   CLOSE-UP OF AN OLD SUITCASE
lying on the floor. Mike's hands come into the SHOT, open up the suitcase. It is filled with war relics: a German helmet, a doughboy's tin hat, a bayonet, etc., and a couple of hand grenades. Mike's hands seize the two hand grenades.

222. LIVING ROOM
Mike comes out of the closet stuffing a hand grenade in each pocket, a look of fierce determination on his face. His brother's fate has turned him into a killer. He jams his hat on his head. PAN with him as he strides across the room. He stops for a moment for a last look at Tom's body, then strides out of the house.

223. POWERS BEDROOM
Mrs. Powers is laying out a dressing gown and slippers beside the bed, singing her Irish song happily. The sound of the song is carried on through the final

FADE OUT

THE END

Notes to the Screenplay

Of the differences between the film and the shooting script, many are alterations of phrasing: for the most part they are in the direction of more natural speech, in general and as appropriate to specific characters. Tom, for example, more often says "ain't," while that slang word is deleted from the more conventional Mike's vocabulary. Usually such changes appear to have been made on the spot by the actors with Wellman's tacit approval, if not at his initiative. The actors often had a more accurate sense of the language of the characters than the academically trained Harvey Thew. In this way, again, they bear out their sense of identification with the characters. It is unnecessary to recapitulate each of the numerous small alterations in detail, but a few examples are given.

All of the more substantive editing is given. The surviving materials usually do not clearly show whether changes were made before or during shooting or in the cutting room, nor do they indicate whether Zanuck's advance approval, required under studio rules, was obtained. (As to cutting, however, Wellman's boast that there was remarkably little wasted footage may be pertinent.) In some instances the Warner Brothers archive at the Wisconsin Center for Film and Theater Research (which includes John Bright and Kubec Glasmon's draft novel and the shooting script, but no intermediate drafts or notes) clarifies the purposes of the alterations; the significant ones are discussed in the Introduction or may be identified below. Caution: Variant prints may exist, perhaps stemming from later re-releases.

1 The dialogue with the girls is omitted. Instead, Matt says, "Give us a little kiss, huh?" The girls march through the doors, which swing back and strike Matt in the mouth. "That's what you get for fooling with women," says Tom.
2 Scenes 16 and 17 are not in the film.
3 As Tom goes up the stairs Matt advises him, "Tell him you were only kiddin', Tom . . . "
4 The beating takes place in a bedroom, not in the kitchen, and is prefaced by Tom's line, "How do ya want 'em this time, up or down?"
5 Putty Nose's song (it is not "Frankie and Johnnie") is heard only

faintly in the background against the talk of the poker players whom Matt and Tom pass on their way in. As the boys approach the piano Putty Nose is singing, "Mrs. Jones, big and fat, / Slipped on the ice and broke her . . . " The boys around the piano respond rowdily.

6 Tom adds, "He's learnin' how to be poor."

7 "Take it off me, will you?" snaps Tom. A moment before, Tom and Matt's nervousness shows as they enter the warehouse: MATT: Gee . . . I'm scared stiff. TOM: Come on. There's nothing to be scared of. MATT: Is that so . . . look at yer . . . yer shakin' yerself.

8 Matt adds, "But Putty Nose got us into this. He promised to see us through."

9 Scene 59 is not in the film.

10 Scenes 77–79 are not in the film.

11 Scenes 81–83 are not in the film. Scene 84 ends here and plays after scene 93 in the film.

12 Scenes 94–98 are not in the film.

13 Tom's measurements (as announced by the tailor) were reduced somewhat to accord more accurately with Cagney's.

14 Scenes 100 and 102 are not in the film.

15 Kitty and Mamie view them with disgust: "A couple of light-weights." "Yeah—flat tires."

16 The preceding speeches, from Paddy's "but it's going to open up," are not in the film.

17 Instead of Pat's line, this dialogue follows:

   PAT: Yeah, and that ain't all. He and Matt have been running with a couple of girls at the Washington Arms Hotel. Well, now the worst part of it all is that he's been lying to his mother. He's leaving her think that he's made an honest success. But sure it's only a question of time when he's gonna be caught—and then he'll be after breakin' her poor heart.

   MIKE: But what's he doing?

   PAT: Beer—bootleg—he's one of Paddy Ryan's gang—but that's not all. Sure they stop at nothing. You either take their beer or they put you on the spot. Ah, I tell you, Michael, it's a wicked business. Why, only last week . . .

18 Cabbage replaces the incongruous sauerkraut. The scene that follows is not in the film.

19 The first three speeches in this scene are not in the film.

20 Instead of "you ain't so good yourself" Tom says, "Besides, your hands ain't so clean."

21 Scene 133 is not in the film and, to maintain a semblance of separate bedrooms in deference to the censors, the beginning of scene 134 offers Nathan's part of the telephone conversation: "Hello. Is Tom there? Well, I just called his apartment and they said he stepped across the hall for breakfast."

22 Tom's reply in the film is more direct: "There you go with that wishin' stuff again. I wish you was a wishin' well—so that I could tie a bucket to you and sink you."

23 Scenes 138 and 139 are not in the film.

24 Gwen's reference to the Congress Hotel as her residence was deleted from later prints of the film in deference to the respectable reputation of that worthy Chicago establishment, at the request of its attorney.

25 Nails has additional lines: "Great, the best is none too good tonight. Matt's decided to take something lawful—a wife. Now, that's something to celebrate about, isn't it?"

26 Scenes 150 and 151 are not in the film.

27 The scene outside the house ends this way (and the first two lines in scene 160 are omitted):

TOM: We got a little business to settle, jane or no jane.

PUTTY NOSE: You ain't sore, are you, Tom? I've always been your friend.

TOM: Sure. You taught us how to cheat, steal, and kill. Then you lammed out on us.

MATT: Yeah. If it hadn't been for you, we might have been on the level.

TOM: Sure, we might have been ding-dings on a streetcar.

28 This exchange between Tom and Matt is not in the film.

29 As in the early scene at the Red Oaks Club, Putty Nose sings that song rather than "Frankie and Johnnie."

30 Scenes 167–69 follow this scene.

31 The dialogue now skips to Tom's "You know, when I met you . . . "

32 This speech is not in the film, nor is scene 166.

33 The dialogue is omitted in this scene.

34 The dialogue in scene 171 and scene 172 to this point is condensed as follows:

PADDY: Right now we ain't got a chance. Since Nails is gone his mob has scattered. They're ten to one against us. Look at this dump. Four pineapples tossed at us in two days. And the brewery set fire. I'm tellin' you they got us on the run.

TOM: Not me. I ain't runnin'. I ain't yellow.

PADDY: Who said you was? I ain't talking about that. I'm going to need you and you won't be no good to me when you're in the cemetery. I've got to have a couple of days to get the boys lined up again. While I'm doing that you're going to be where nobody knows where to find you, except me. Come on, give me your guns and your money—all of it.

TOM: What are you trying to pull, Paddy?

PADDY: I'm going to keep you off the streets. Even you wouldn't be sap enough to go for a stroll without your gat. Come on. Shower down. All of it. All of it.

TOM: You got a phone here, Jane? I'm going to call Gwen.

35 Hack speaks: "Yards 6321. Hello. Is Schemer there?"

36 Jane's lines in the film (from Tom's "Naw, I don't need any help") are: "Be a good boy and sit down. I'll take your shoes off, too. I want to do things for you, Tommy. You don't think I'm old, do you, Tommy? You like me, don't you, Tommy?" The dialogue transcript of the film shows that Tom had additional lines at the end of the scene that were deleted from the film (at the time of original release or to secure code office approval for re-release in 1937 or 1952): "Ah, in your hat. Ah, get away from me. You're Paddy Ryan's girl."

37 Dialogue added at the end of the scene:

MATT: Hey, Tom, wait a minute. What happened?

TOM: Aw, nothing. I just got burned up, that's all.

MATT: What do you want to run out on me for? We're together, ain't we?

TOM: Sure.

38 Scenes 192–94 are not in the film. Some prints may contain a shot of Tom finding Gwen's apartment empty and leaving it, quickly and expressionlessly.

39 The .45-caliber pistol is reduced, inappropriately, to a .38.

40 Groaning and coughing, Tom collapses and says, "I ain't so tough." This addition was undoubtedly another concession to anticipated censors.

41 The first part of this speech is not in the film, nor is the first part of his first speech (through "I was the sucker . . . not Mike") in this scene.

42 Mrs. Powers adds, "And he'll be coming home soon, won't he?" "Sure, Ma," replies Mike.

43 The remaining scenes are not in the film. In the final shot the arm of a phonograph grinds away at the end of a record.

Production Credits

Directed by	William A. Wellman
Story by	Kubec Glasmon and John Bright
Screenplay by	Harvey Thew
Photography by	Dev Jennings
Art Director	Max Parker
Edited by	Ed McCormick
Wardrobe by	Earl Luick
Vitaphone Orchestra conducted by	David Mendota

Released: May 1931
Running time: 96 minutes

Cast

Tom Powers	James Cagney
Gwen Allen	Jean Harlow
Matt Doyle	Edward Woods
Mamie	Joan Blondell
Ma Powers	Beryl Mercer
Mike Powers	Donald Cook
Kitty	Mae Clarke
Jane	Mia Marvin
Nails Nathan	Leslie Fenton
Paddy Ryan	Robert Emmett O'Connor
Putty Nose	Murray Kinnell
Bugs Moran	Ben Hendricks, Jr.
Molly Doyle	Rita Flynn
Dutch	Clark Burroughs
Hack Miller	Snitz Edwards
Mrs. Doyle	Adele Watson
Tom as a boy	Frank Coghlan, Jr.
Matt as a boy	Frankie Darro
Officer Powers	Purnell Pratt

Inventory

The following materials from the Warner Library of the Wisconsin Center for Film and Theater Research were used by Cohen in preparing *The Public Enemy* for the Wisconsin/Warner Bros. Screenplay Series:

Novel (typescript), "Beer and Blood: The Story of a Couple o' Wrong Guys," by Kubec Glasmon and John Bright. No date. 348 pages.
Final screenplay, by Harvey Thew. January 18, 1931. 134 pages.

DESIGNED BY GARY GORE
COMPOSED BY GRAPHIC COMPOSITION, INC.
ATHENS, GEORGIA
MANUFACTURED BY FAIRFIELD GRAPHICS
FAIRFIELD, PENNSYLVANIA
TEXT AND DISPLAY LINES ARE SET IN PALATINO

Library of Congress Cataloging in Publication Data
Thew, Harvey.
The public enemy.
(Wisconsin/Warner Bros. screenplay series)
Screenplay by Harvey Thew.
Bibliography: pp. 34–35.
I. Cohen, Henry, 1933–
II. Wisconsin Center for Film and Theater Research.
III. Public enemy. [Motion picture]   IV. Series.
PN1997.P797   812'.52   80-52292
ISBN 0-299-08460-4
ISBN 0-299-08464-7 (pbk.)

The Wisconsin/Warner Bros. Screenplay Series, a product of the Warner Brothers Film Library of the University of Wisconsin-Madison, offers scholars, students, researchers, and aficionados insights into individual films that have never before been possible.

The Warner library was acquired in 1957 by the United Artists Corporation, which in turn donated it to the Wisconsin Center for Film and Theater Research in 1969. The massive library, housed in the State Historical Society of Wisconsin, contains eight hundred sound feature films, fifteen hundred short subjects, and nineteen thousand still negatives, as well as the legal files, press books, and screenplays of virtually every Warner film produced from 1930 until 1950. This rich treasure trove has made the University of Wisconsin one of the major centers for film research, attracting scholars from around the world. This series of published screenplays represents a creative use of the Warner library, both a boon to scholars and a tribute to United Artists.

Most published film scripts are literal transcriptions of finished films. The Wisconsin/Warner screenplays are primary source documents—the final shooting versions including revisions made during production. As such, they reveal the art of screenwriting as other film transcriptions cannot. Comparing these screenplays with the final films will illuminate the arts of directing and acting, as well as the other arts of the film making process. (Films of the Warner library are available at modest rates from the United Artists nontheatrical rental library, United Artists/16 mm.)

From the eight hundred feature films in the library, the editors of the series selected for publication examples that have received critical recognition for excellence of directing, screenwriting, and acting, films distinctive in genre, in historical relevance, and in adaptation of well-known novels and plays.